Introduction

The English Parish Church is often though
in a fast changing world, a place of peace a
counterbalance to all that is uncertain. In
been a focus of conflict and change: change
approved or acceptable opinions and practic
and enmities of the last thousand years of E   .... stones of St.
Mary's, in their present beauty and prayerfulness, bear, like all churches, the
marks and scars of that history; and what has left no marks they have
silently witnessed.

Most Christians take church buildings for granted; yet they are not primary
or even essential to the faith. The Church, as clergy sometimes like to
remind congregations, is a body of people. The earliest church buildings
post date the first Pentecost by two centuries and were adapted houses. That
communities devoted so much attention over centuries to the elaboration
and beautification of buildings says something about the form of their belief
in God, about the holiness of particular places, about the visible forms by
which an invisible God can be represented. That individuals gave of their
substance (and sometimes of their small change) to the church may say
something about their priorities or about their fears and desire to obtain
favour, even about their guilt.

Sometimes the church was the glue that held communities together; sometimes it was the source of division or sometimes its emblem. Individual conscience and a community identity apply contrary pressures. These different experiences are reflected in the pages that follow.

However, the interaction between faith and daily living over time is difficult to pin down. Some histories of village life are written as if the inhabitants believed nothing or were actuated purely by economic motives. Some describe what happened to and in church buildings without reference to how people earned their bread or conducted their working lives. It seems very unlikely that either of these descriptions would be recognisable to the villagers. On the other hand it is very difficult to achieve any understanding of what people thought and how it affected their lives unless they recorded both. This rarely happened. Written records are most often about money, about what was supposed to happen and about those occasions when things went wrong. It is, of course, harder to detect the local impact of big events. Meanwhile, in reaching their conclusions some historians have sunnier dispositions than others.

Theology itself does not stand still. The questions posed by a Palestinian Jewish sub-culture were not the same in all respects as those raised by mediaeval kingdoms, whether in their internal organisation, in jockeying for power between themselves or when threatened by alien invasion. Attempts to meet new situations with fresh but authentic thinking were sometimes made in conditions of calm, often when faced with challenge and under pressure. What is a legitimate development and what a distortion of Christ's gospel will always be a matter of dispute; what is the lesser evil may be clearer with hindsight, but unhappily the corruptibility of human purposes is a weighty factor in such matters.

In what follows, the story is partly about the village; partly about its context. It may seem that South Creake is only a peg on which to hang the larger story. On the contrary, generalities depend on particular places and for most of our period most people lived in villages, on which the few but increasing numbers of towns depended for both food and raw materials and for their populations. Until the eighteenth century the capacity of Norwich to consume human lives would have left it desolate without its being continually fed with people from the countryside[1]. Villages were a vital resource both of people and food; they were not, as we shall see, self-contained and isolated units; labourers moved in search of work, soldiers were recruited, land was bought and sold, ideas were disseminated; they may not have been the places where ideas originated but they were the places where some of them were practised.

Finally, human life is about belonging as well as striving and a village can be seen as a laboratory in which the capacity of human beings to belong and their failure to do so can be tested.

Beginnings – Invasion and Assimilation (1066- 1300)

St. Mary's, South Creake is a parish within the diocese of Norwich, close to the north Norfolk coast, now part of a benefice of five churches, one of nine parishes of the ancient Brothercross Hundred[2]. The parochial system, which we take for granted, (though it is increasingly under threat from the shortage of clergy) evolved only gradually. A considerable impetus to its development, however, was the Norman invasion, which therefore seems a good place to start.

The arrival of Christianity in these parts pre-dates the Conquest. East Anglia had been part of the diocese of Elmham since the seventh century. The Saxon church functioned through a series of large missionary churches, or minsters, around which were a series of satellite churches, but the coverage that this provided was less than complete and alongside the system private chapels or oratories developed, possibly as a response to the ninth century Viking invasions which had considerably weakened the older institutions[3]. These proprietary chapels owed no allegiance to the minsters and initially little to bishops, but the effect of their appearance was to place a priest in every village. The payment of tithe, the biblical tenth, long recognised, was made compulsory in the reign of King Edgar (959-75) thus putting them on a more secure footing.

---

[1] Births did not exceed deaths in Norwich until the mid late eighteenth century: *Population 1700-1950,* Alan Armstrong in *Norwich since 1550* (Continuum 2005) p. 249

[2] At the time of the Domesday Survey it was in Gallow Hundred and was subsequently transferred. The Hundred was an administrative unit of Saxon origin which became progressively obsolete and finally ceased to exist in the 19th.century.

[3] *The Parish churches of Medieval England,* Colin Platt (Secker and Warburg 1981) p. 1

The arrival of the Norman was a shock not only because of the innovations they made but because of the manner of their governance. Duke William claimed legitimacy as the lawful successor of Edward; he also asserted his ownership of all land in England and his subjects as his tenants, from the highest baron to the lowliest serf, thus dispossessing the Saxon landowners to a man. From the very beginning, there was resistance all over the country, including, of course, the fens, which lasted for years after the conquest. The local people were often treated with disdain sometimes with savagery – it has been said that the Normans ruled by terror[4]. The invaders, in turn, met with revolt after revolt. William's thoroughness and brilliance as a campaigner finally routed the opposition of earls on the one hand and the irregular *silvatici* – guerrillas in our language – on the other. The old English elites were almost completely destroyed[5]; local landowners, like Bondi were either killed or exiled; in either case they were dispossessed. All of which makes the reconciliation and assimilation of the two peoples so remarkable.

[4] *The English and the Normans,* Hugh M. Thomas (Oxford 2003) p. 168
[5] Ibid. p. 59-60

The first voices we hear are not local, but they may well have been reflected in what some people hereabouts thought. Theirs was a very old question: why did God allow the success of the invasion. It is also a modern question; in their case, they were not asking it in terms of personal tragedy, but political change. One answer to the question as to why God had allowed the Conquest to succeed was that the English and not only King Harold had done something wrong so as to deserve divine punishment[6]. This was a view shared between both Norman and English writers, such as Henry of Huntingdon and even the monk Aelred of Rievaulx. It made the task of re-asserting the integrity and dignity of the natives a harder task; in addressing it the role of the pious king Edward the Confessor, who had died just before the conquest, became important; he had, according to his first biographer, claimed that God's anger would end only when the two thrones, English and Norman were united, as they were in the reign of Henry I (1100-1135). More than this would be required.

The Normans needed the English. They claimed to be the rightful inheritors of the land but they constituted only a very small part of the population. While they showed themselves more than capable of putting down revolts, maintaining the productivity of the land was a different matter. South Creake was already a village with an organised agriculture, its field system long divided into arable strips[7], surrounded by heath and woodland above the little river valley in which it was set. The newcomers were not welcome; moreover, their new administration did not so much make systematic plans as record what was there: most of the arable and pasture were to the north and west of the village where the land was better. The south of the village was heath and rough pasture. The various manors, Saxon in origin, each owned strips of land in various parts of the village; the system had been in existence for several centuries[8]. The Domesday survey of 1086, whose purpose was the recording of everything of value for taxation purposes, records the manorial grants as at that date: the king held personally one manor, a second was held by Hugh de Montfort, a third by the hugely rich and influential Earl William de Warenne, within which was a church with five acres of land[9]. That it had land may have been the reason for including

[6] Thomas (2003) p. 243

[7] Many of the fields survive to this day: *Medieval Field Systems and Land Tenure in South Creake,* Mary Hesse Norfolk Archaeology vol. XLIII (1998) p. 81

[8] Ibid. p. 83

[9] *A History of Norfolk* , ed. William Page, (Victoria County History 1906) p. 91

it, for often churches were not mentioned; nearby churches at Waterden, Sculthorpe and Barmer are among the few recorded in the Survey.

The king's manor, subsequently to become the principle manor of the village was granted, sometime after the Domesday survey, by Henry I (1100-1135)[10] to Ralf de Beaufoe (or Bello Fago) of Pont l'Evêque. The family had been at the battle of Hastings and their English holdings were extensive.

The manor appears to have had a church also. For in 1180 Ralph, the son of the first Ralph of Beaufoe, gave the rectory with its tithes, lands and homages to Castle Acre Priory, 'for the soul's health of King Henry I who had brought him up and that of his Lord King Henry II, his grandson'[11]. It is the first local voice we hear, albeit formally written, probably by a clerk on his behalf, an act of gratitude directed not to his benefactor but to the God who had made this happen and whose mercy he now sought for the soul of the late King. Thomas, his brother confirmed the gift in 1181, probably on the death of the former. Whatever happened to the Warenne church it was Beaufoes' little chapel, probably built of wood which appears to have survived, built uphill from the manor house which stood between the church and the river[12].

Castle Acre thus became the fourth manor, acquiring other manorial rights by various gifts from such as the Candos family from 1192 onwards. It had been founded from the French monastery at Cluny between 1087 and 1089 at the invitation of the Earl Warenne[13]; the French connection was typical. Yet what began as the expression of colonialism, over time weakened and changed its character. There were many factors at work in bringing about the assimilation: practically, there was the downward mobility of the younger sons of the Normans and the upward mobility particularly of the very lowest among the English; and the usefulness of English officials to the invaders. In addition, English propaganda in defence of their historical pedigree[14] was influential; as was the contracting of strategic marriages, not least that of Henry I to an English princess, to which Edward's prophecy

[10] *An Essay toward a Topographical History of Norfolk,* Francis Blomefield and Charles Parkin vol. vii (1806) p.78; Hesse (1998) p. 82
[11] Blomefield ((1806) p.83
[12] Ibid. p. 3-4; Graham Pooley, *Eleven Hundred Years* (Fakenham 1980) p. 63 Aerial photographs revealed its likely location.
[13] Page (1906) vol. 2 p.356
[14] Cf. *The Deeds of the English kings,* William of Malmsbury (1095-1143)

was held to refer, but another was that the Normans and Saxons were of the same religion using a common language, Latin. Cluny was, of course, the centre of an important and well-organised reformed system of Benedictine houses based in France and visitors from Cluny came routinely to inspect its houses; the relationship was at once local and international, therefore ambiguous. The monks were English and until the events leading up to the Hundred Years' War (1339-1453) England included much of France (during which war English houses such as Castle Acre were subject to interference and deprivation. Only in 1373 was Castle Acre 'denizened', declared to be an English house, thus ending the disputes over who should appoint the clergy and what should become of its income.)

The invaders had brought their clergy with them; but from an early date many parish priests were English. By 1101, Nearby Binham Priory had a majority of priests, who functioned in parishes, with English names[15]. For whereas it was politic to appoint Normans to bishoprics and abbacies, where English talents could be employed without serious risk natives were appointed; one reason was there were not enough French clergy to go round, but the theory that they were of the same church (and William the rightful inheritor of the throne) was also matched by practice and at a number of levels attempts were made to break down barriers.

By the late twelfth century, the process of assimilation had been largely achieved: church and kingdom were seen as two expressions of the *patria,* the nation[16]. French and English monks shared the same life, and because they were expected to exercise moral leadership in medieval society, the bonds of friendship between them were strongly influential[17]. This ran from the top: Anselm, archbishop and Benedictine monk, expressed by his words and the conduct of his friendships across the divide, his belief in the superiority of Christian love in breaking down barriers: his biographer, Eadmer, was an Englishman. The monasteries owed their position to the nobility and in turn administered land on which villages stood; they bridged what was a great divide. Castle Acre Priory received lands from men like Ulph with Saxon names as well as from Normans. Gradually, the Normans became English.

---

[15] Thomas (2003) p. 210

[16] Ibid. p. 285; after the murder of Thomas Becket at the behest of Henry II.

[17] Ibid. p. 219

The Normans were also a warrior people who celebrated their warfare even in churches. Norman Architecture is redolent of images of soldiers and battles. In a Europe devoid of nation states in the modern sense, Christendom had been subject to threat by an aggressive and proselytising Islam which, since the seventh century had captured the holy places, invaded North Africa and Spain and threatened France; by the eleventh century the Normans, 'with a surplus of arms-bearers and a insufficiency of land'[18] were among those who had set about pushing back the tide. Norman England was part of this same Christendom and thus became caught up in the religious response in what became known as the Crusades. Pope Urban II (1035-1099), a former prior of Cluny, rallied France to arms with a preaching tour intended to send soldiers to recover the holy places including Jerusalem, now in the hands of the Seljuk Turks. This was a holy war not a just war. When William of Normandy had invaded England at Hastings, though this was justified because Harold was an oath breaker, nevertheless his knights had to do penance for their slaughtering. Urban now made acts of carnage by those who took up the cross themselves into acts of penance. The crusader did not do penance for taking up arms; the act of taking up arms was itself an act of penance. The first Crusade was a French affair wreathed in myth, and it was out of the mythology which confused pilgrimage with holy war that subsequently, in the Second and Third Crusades, Norfolk men like Earl Warenne and William of Cley[19] took the cross. Knights required a retinue from their households, sometimes large in number, and Norfolk men no doubt were recruited as they would throughout the ages as seamen or soldiers. Crusaders themselves, those who had taken the vow, were mostly drawn from knightly or merchant classes; the contribution of villagers otherwise was in taxation, such as the Saladin tithe of 1188 or Lord Edwards's tax of 1270.

The principle of crusading, that of a response to the call to repentance and the offer of salvation was normative; its practice in warfare has been a matter of dispute, one historian regarding it as 'the sin against the Holy Ghost', others as a logical expression of a warrior society in defence of Christendom: '…if knights were forbidden to pursue their profession within Christendom, then just causes outside had to be found.' [20] It is a reminder

---

[18] *God's War – a New history of the Crusades,* C.J. Tyerman (Allen Lane 2000) p. 13-14

[19] *England and the Crusades,* C.J. Tyerman (Chicago 1988) p. 216

[20] *History of the Crusades,* Steven Runciman (Cambridge 1951-4) vol. 3, p. 480; Tyerman (2006) p. 44

that the explication of the faith in widely different social settings entails decisions and actions sometimes at variance with each other.

The relationship between parishes and monasteries was complex. Monastic houses relied upon the income from the parish churches which they owned in order to survive. St. Mary's was one of twenty six churches belonging to Castle Acre. The tithe was paid in kind, whether as hay or wheat, milk, cheese, poultry, eggs; iron ore and stone; the products of fisheries; even the value of goods made[21]. This comprehensive means of taxation went mostly to the patron, in this case Castle Acre; a small portion of it that often most difficult to collect was paid to the local priest.

On the other hand, there were perceived advantages to the arrangement: some spiritual; some material. The twelfth century was a time of great monastic reform and of religious enthusiasm. The cult of the Blessed Virgin and the saints had become popular[22]. The churches of the benefice as it now is, North and South Creake, Syderstone, Sculthorpe and Waterden, are typical in that four of them are dedicated to the Virgin and one to All Saints and one to both. The prayers of monks were held to be of more value than that of mere secular clergy and the life of prayer, whether practised by monks or hermits, hugely appreciated.

A second advantage was more visible. Castle Acre was instrumental in replacing wooden churches with stone as, for instance, in Sutton in Lincolnshire when they took over ownership; it may have been they who set about the rebuilding of South Creake church. The twelfth century church, (of which almost nothing remains) was most probably a simple affair, heavy and dark, as Norman architecture then was. (A few feet of the lower part of the chancel arch is said to date from early Plantagenet times, 1180-1200, together with the jambs of a window on the south side to the east of the priest's door).[23] It would have consisted of one or at most two 'rooms': one for the congregation and one for the altar and the clergy, the liturgical space. Modest, though it may have been by later standards, it was nevertheless the most significant building in the parish, matched if at all by the manor house and the mill.

---

[21] *A History of the English Parish,* N.J.G. Pounds (Cambridge 2000) p. 208ff.
[22] Platt (1981) p. 7-8; Bernard of Clairvaux (1090-1153) was the great proponent of her cult as well as a critic of monastic laxity; while at Cluny, a target of criticisms, the abbot Peter the Venerable (1092-1156) was responsible for the abbey's reform.
[23] Pooley (1980) p. 9

As for what went on inside, we know this in part from the instructions of Bishop Quinel of Exeter of 1287 which set out the minimal requirements. They included a small chalice of silver or silver gilt and a ciborium to hold the sacramental bread and for the visitation of the sick. The church will have had a silver chrismatory for the holy oils, a censer and an incense boat; with a pax brede, (a tablet engraved with an image of Christ to be kissed at the peace), and three cruets and a holy water vessel; it must have had a pyx (a little box of ivory or silver for the reserved sacrament) and another for the unconsecrated bread. There would be one altar of stone, fixed and immoveable with its cloths, canopy and frontal; there would have been a fixed font of stone (securely locked to prevent misuse of the baptismal water); and there were to be two images, one of the patron saint of the church and the other of the Virgin Mary – in our case they were the same. For special services and for processions, the candlesticks and crosses should include a multiple candleholder for the Holy Week services, known as a *tenebrae,* with a paschal candlestick, again for Easter, two processional tapers and two great crosses, one of which had to be portable. Other items would be needed for weddings and funerals, vestments for festivals and ordinary Sundays, and a considerable number of books[24]. Regular inspections – visitations, as they were called - took place to ensure that things were in order, and often they were not. St. Mary's church may have been one of many which relied on cast-off monastic books or old ones cheaply bought.

It was a very visual religion, centring on the two great sacraments of Baptism and the Mass, both administered only by the duly ordained priest, both also having become hugely elaborated from the practice of washing and eating together from which they partly derived to express the sharing in Christ's atoning sacrifice: the first allowing entry into the community of those saved by baptism into his death expressed by the total immersion of the infant; the second the participation in his life by sharing in his sacramental body and blood under the forms of bread and wine. Because the latter were surrounded by symbols of purity, holiness and awe, they came more regularly to be viewed rather than consumed.

Only a minority of people could read; it was one of the marks of the clergy that they were able to. The expensive books which a parish must buy included the instructions, both liturgical and catechetical, which a priest must follow. Archbishop Pecham's instructions of 1281 were a much copied

---

[24] Platt (1981) p. 27

model. Apart from telling the priest what must be done in church, particularly in Holy Week, he was to teach (to be memorised by the people) the Fourteen Articles of Faith, Ten Commandments of the law (and the two of the gospel), the seven works of mercy, the seven deadly sins, the seven virtues and the seven sacraments. Confessions were to be made at least annually[25] a development which resulted in the proliferation of manuals to guide the clergy in instructing their people. The language of the church was Latin, that of educated folk and of the manorial courts French (until the mid fourteenth century) whereas common folk spoke English, in which tongue increasingly they were taught[26].

The clergy, or at least some of them, were recruited locally, indicating the existence of some form of schooling hereabouts, possibly monastic. Most schooling had ordination in view and its importance was stressed by the Third and Fourth Lateran councils (1179 & 1215). Their final training may have taken place at Castle Acre. On the other hand Rudham, eight miles away, had a grammar school run by the Augustinian canons of Coxford[27]. Walsingham, another Augustinian house, was closer, and had a monastic school[28] from which latterly scholars were sent to the university. The Augustinians were noted for their interest in education. The children of villeins – serfs - were effectively excluded from education; free tenants were not. Parish clerks, assistants to the clergy, some but not all of whom became clergy themselves, often became teachers of small children[29]; some were taught at home by their mothers. Literacy, as a means of advancement, was desired by some and feared by others.

Parochial clergy were much a part of their communities. A good number of clergy though they held benefices were absentees, being administrators or scholars, leaving behind lowly paid curates; these parish priests were often the less intellectual but they were not thereby less pastorally adept; in any case they lived by the tithes they received and the land they farmed. The tithe was always likely to be a matter of dispute which, according to

---

[25] Platt (1981) p. 48; following the Fourth Lateran Council in 1215: *The Stripping of the Altars,* Eamon Duffy (Yale 1992) p. 54
[26]*Medieval Schools,* Nicholas Orme *(*Yale 2006) p. 219
[27]Orme *(* 2006) p. 193
[28] The visitation of 1526 notes the failure to send scholars to the university, implying that this had been and should be the case: Page (1906) p. 396
[29] Orme (2006) p. 208

contemporary advice[30], had to be dealt with 'cautiously and discreetly' so as to prevent discord between priest and parishioners. Vicarages, built by patron monastic houses, go back at least to the thirteenth century. Celibacy was imposed on clergy from the eleventh century but it was slow to take hold; housekeepers were often 'hearth mates' and a few incumbencies were de facto hereditary until the practice was either brought to an end or driven underground. Among clerical tasks was that of moderating between the 'likely tyrannies of both manorial lord and over-wealthy villein'; it was not only those outside the church who were critical of abuses, whether clerical or lay[31]. Thus, a confessor's manual of the day advises penance on lords who exact more than is their due; confessions, which were to be made at least annually, allowed the priest not merely to hear but to interrogate a penitent[32]. All of this suggests the development of a caste of clergy answerable to bishops as well as to their manorial lord.

Another function of literacy was that from the early thirteenth century the courts of the four manors which possessed land in the village recorded their proceedings in writing. Records came to be kept of the transactions of the courts: reports of agricultural yields, payments made, the settlement of disputes, and even peasant land transfers[33]. This was partly an accounting process but was also a means of ensuring good order within the community. Every six weeks or so every householder was required by the lord to attend and to assist in the judgement of the cases of the various suitors[34]. Most people were tied to the land by their allegiance to their lord via the manorial courts and by the laws which prevented villeins from leaving their village without permission. Three fifths of the population in the late thirteenth century was of unfree status. The lord relied upon the villagers as much as they on him; he needed them to work the land he farmed himself, his demesne; it was important that they believed that justice was being done. The difference between free and unfree tenants was that the former knew the extent of their obligations to the lord whereas the latter did not; from seasonal work such as ploughing, sowing and reaping, to the weekly obligations – carting dung, weeding, threshing, scouring ditches, trimming hedges and mending fences – 'whatever the lord wills'. 'Boon works', extra

---

[30] *Regimen animarum* (1343) quoted in Platt (1981) p. 56

[31] Platt (1981) pp. 53, 50

[32] *Memoriale Presbyterorum* (1344) quoted in *The English Church in the Fourteenth Century* W.A. Pantin (Cambridge 1955) p. 208;

[33] *From Memory to Written Record 1066-1307*, M. Clanchy (Blackwell 1993) p. 50

[34] *Life on the English Manor 1150-1400*, H.S. Bennett (Cambridge 1937) p. 203f

demands of the lord sometimes took them from their own small plots. Only sickness, Sundays and the holy days of the church freed them from the cycle of toil and even the latter were not always observed, even by monastic landlords[35]. Fortunately, a day's work was usually defined by the tasks to be performed, which often meant only half a day. The village was prosperous compared with many; Norfolk was the bread basket of the nation. Wheat and barley were grown; sheep provided both wool and milk and fertilised the arable; pigs inhabited the woods.

Those who fell on hard times, widows and orphans, even the aged and infirm, might hope for some support from the almonry of Creake abbey a mile or so to the north. Its elevation to the status of Abbey owed much to its popularity as a place to which 'many needy folk flock, the best refuge for those oppressed by great misery'. Unlike many former hospitals, it appears to have continued its care for poor men after its elevation to the status of Abbey, (though, like many Augustinian houses, it fell on bad times later.). It had been founded as a hospital in 1206 in and became an Augustinian Abbey in 1231. It acquired de Montfort's manor now called Bodham's, by a series of grants in or about 1287 made by William de Bodham; its original foundation having been made by Alice, widow of Robert de Nerford, Constable of Dover castle[36].

The other manors were Beaufoes, the principal manor of the village, and Castle Acre manor as already described. Finally, Earl Warenne's lands, part of which had been held from him by the freeman Lambert de Rosee at the Survey, were expanded in the time of his descendant Baldwin in the twelfth century as Rose's Manor. His holdings had become considerable and included a mill, a most valuable item of property – villagers had to pay to have their corn milled and the ownership of hand mills was prohibited. Rose's Manor retained its name even though part of it came into the hands of Castleacre priory, and part to the Calthorp family of Burnham[37]. Because of the division of the land between the manors in the village (and the growth of the number of free tenants) some negotiation between them would have been necessary[38].

[35] Bennett (1937) p. 112ff.

[36] *Cartulary of Creake Abbey,* A.L.Bedingfield (Norfolk Records Society 1966) p.xv

[37] Blomefield (1806) p. 80

[38] Hesse (1998) p. 82

If the manorial courts regulated matters relating to the land, the bishop's and archdeacon's court regulated ecclesiastic and personal matters. The latter met in the nearest convenient church. Actions ranged from neglect of the church fabric to adultery, slander or marriage within the proscribed limits; and less contentiously the proving of wills[39]. The penalties imposed were the performance of a public penance for minor infringements, excommunication for more serious offences. In 1317, two girls of the village, Alice Herlle and Alice Gutermound, were sentenced by the rural dean 'to a penance of seven whippings around the church' on pain of excommunication should they refuse for unnamed offences which they had confessed[40]. Religion was mediated through the whole community of South Creake, in which family, friends, clergy and the saints in heaven were all a part.

It was a time of prosperity: population was rising, harvests were good, epidemics were rare and markets everywhere were proliferating. When times were less good, the problems which monastic ownership produced would become more acute; inevitably the taking of money from the parish was likely to produce abuses and reforming bishops had an interest in limiting the power of monasteries.

Hard times – poverty, war, disease and revolt (1300-1400)

By the late thirteenth century there was a reaction against monastic influence. The statutes of Mortmain 1279 and 1290 were intended to prevent land coming into the hands of the church, effectively monasteries, which did not pay tax. Those, therefore, who wished to provide for the welfare of their souls, were more likely to put their money during their lifetimes into the parish church, particularly those who had benefited from the Crusades by being given land in exchange for their subsidy. The Statute of Exeter of 1287 encouraged this by laying the responsibility for the nave upon the parishioners. Thus, the chancel with its Y tracery windows is reckoned to have rebuilt towards the end of the thirteenth century, including the piscina and even the chancel arch. (The large south window is clearly much later). The pointed arch, borrowed from Islamic architecture via the Crusades, was more flexible in its dimensions than the semi-circular arch leading first to the tall slim lancet windows of the Early English, and then, as here in South Creake, the transitional period which, by 1300, led to new lighter styles of

---

[39] Pounds (2000) p. 296ff.
[40] *Ecclesiastical Discipline at South Creake in 1317,* Norfolk Archeology vol. xxiii p. 305

building, more adventurous, more fluent – what came to be known as the Decorated style. Glass was becoming cheaper. The style was thus characterised by larger windows with ornate tracery and narrower, elegant multi-shafted pillars which sometimes rose seamlessly to the arch mouldings without capitals[41], as here.

At some point the chancel was extended by some twelve feet, as is indicated by the changes in the stonework and the intersecting tracery of the east window. But then the work appears to have stopped. The earlier years of the new century, but especially the second decade, 1315, 1316 and 1321 were marked by appalling weather, wet summers resulting in poor harvests, poverty and disease which brought many to the point of starvation. The better harvests following 1322 may have led to the resumption of the work; the aisles, with their reticulated east and west windows, are more advanced than the chancel east window, as is the porch and the tower. The nave, its roof steep and possibly thatched, was built. The tower with its parapet (now lost)[42] was completed. The south porch dates from this period, incorporating the flint flush work for which East Anglia is justly famous. (The statue in the niche between the Marian monograms is modern.) The interruptions tell us two things: that only in good times can people find the means to express themselves beyond their basic needs; but what they spent their money on tells us what they thought was important.

With regard to the chancel, as being the place in which the Eucharist was celebrated, partly seen, partly concealed, its elaboration is understandable; the nave provided for the people; a tower carried the bells calling people to worship in an age without clocks, its mass dial, a primitive clock on the wall telling the priest or clerk when to ring them. The porch, by contrast, seems

---

[41] *The Mediaeval Styles of the English Parish Church*, F.E. Howard (Batsford 1936) p. 73
[42] Remains of the parapet have been detected on the east churchyard wall. No satisfactory account of its loss has been produced.

an indulgence, too large merely to keep the rain off those entering the building. In fact, it was the place of various liminal functions: where marriages were celebrated – followed by a mass in church; where women were churched after childbirth, and where those making public penance were required to wait before doing so in church; it may even have been the place to which the destitute might resort if they had no other accommodation[43]. As such it was an important negotiating point between the world and the things of God.

Whatever works were in progress we can we sure that the advent of the Black Death – bubonic plague – in 1349 brought building as much else to a juddering halt. A population weakened by years of bad harvests in many places in Norfolk was reduced by as much as a half; and the disease recurred in 1361 and was to remain endemic for decades to come. Two generations of the lords of Beaufoes, one a minor, appear to have died in the plague years[44]. Nor was priesthood exempt from this scything down process; the parish had three incumbents that year: Robert Godwin, Edmund Clerk and John atte Grene. We know nothing of these men but in general those who replaced the dead were often illiterate, and if they could read lacked understanding of what they read. Such was the shortage that even such unqualified clergy felt able to demand higher and higher stipends, adding to the woes of common people. Many sought solace as much from spells and incantations as from prayers; religion was at a low ebb. Meanwhile, absentee monastic landlords came in for increasing criticism, while monastic appropriations of parishes continued apace in spite of protests from the bishops. Some monastic institutions even failed to appoint and pay clergy. It is not certain that John atte Grene ever came to the parish. He exchanged his post with that of Burnham Norton in 1354, a procedure known as 'chop-church' by which absentees raised money by receiving the capitalised value of the richer benefice which they gave up and then paying an untenured priest to do the actual job in the new parish[45]. The exchange between John Goleth and William Balle in 1404 may have been another example of the same process. Treating vicarages as sources of revenue did not of course improve pastoral care.

---

[43] Pounds (2000) p.387-8; *The Self-Contained Village?* ed. C. Dyer, article by Stephen Hindle p. 52-3. Poor people were known to live in the porch.

[44] Hesse (1998) p. 86

[45] *English Historical Documents 1327-1485*, A.R. Myers (Routledge 1995) p. 605; *The Churches of Norfolk – Hundred of Brothercross,* Bryant T. Hugh, (Norwich (Mercury 1914) pp.31 & 175

The Hundred Years' War must also have had its effects not only on alien monasteries. Although only a small amount of time was spent actually fighting and all of that on French soil it harmed trade, especially the wool trade with Flanders on which East Anglia much relied, as well as raising taxes. It also drew men into armed service apparently 'from every village in England', to fight Edward III's wars[46]. (By the time his son Richard II came to the throne, the failures of the war had reduced the king to resisting French raids on the south coast.)

The effects of the plague included the loosening of the control of the manors; it also increased the mobility of labour and allowed a turnover in properties which, by the fifteenth century, had become quite rapid. There was a considerable migration of population: few family names persist from 13th century documents to the 1475 or 1559 terriers[47]. Wills indicate a variety of origins of the inhabitants, Norman and Saxon, from nearby, like Rudham or further afield like Nottingham; a few are occupational names like Barker. These, of course, were the folk with enough property to leave by will. With the slackening of the hold of the manorial system local initiative and the accumulation of land by free tenants and their employment of day labour became significant; some fenced their land giving them exclusive use an issue which was eventually to become divisive but which allowed them to develop new farming methods; many unfree tenants – villeins who were bound to their lord to work as he demanded on the demesne – simply moved elsewhere where they were free from his authority. Continuity of village life was provided by those who had a material interest in staying, which the poor did not have[48]. This, in turn produced another change, that in favour of sheep farming by the gentry as being much less labour intensive.

The post-plague years were ones of radical discontinuity but also of persistence. Not a few villages, recorded in Domesday, had simply disappeared; the rebuilding of Cley church was apparently abandoned. Memory in some places died. Yet the Episcopal Visitation in the summer of 1368 instituted by the bishop of Norwich and undertaken by William de Swynflete, his archdeacon, for which only that for the Norwich

---

[46] Bennett (1937) p.124

[47] Hesse (1998) p.86. Terriers were registers of land holdings held by the manors.

[48] Ibid; Dyer (2007) p. 27

archdeaconry survives[49] reveals some places not quite in disarray. Nearby Great Walsingham was recorded as having pretty much a full set of vestments, cloths, vessels, banners and other accoutrements, much as in bishop Quinel's list. Mystics, like Dame Julian of Norwich, lived through the plague to write her revelations on the Passion, to be succeeded by the loquacious Margery Kempe of Lynn. (Both of their works are still in print).

It was also the century of William Langland, author of *Piers Plowman*. His is not a local voice – he came from around Malvern – nor was he a mystic. He does however give us a clue both as the shortcomings of religious observance – lazy bishops, avaricious priests and friars – as well as weak kings, grasping barons and thieving lawyers; but he also sets out a vision of what religion should, in his view, be. Unlike Margery Kempe he wants no

pilgrimages: it is enough to be going the round of one's own parish, seeking God who is Truth and Christ whose face is in everyman[50], who sees those who 'suffer with hunger, with woe in winter…[with] many mouths to eat the pennies up'. As for the penitential system 'though ye be a brother of all the Orders five, though ye have a pocket full of pardons

and absolutions…unless Do–well help you your patents and your pardons will be worth – a piecrust'[51]. Well-versed in scripture he is critical (and in some respects his criticisms foreshadow those of the Reformers) yet he is no radical: he criticises 'wastrels' (rebels) who will not work as well as knights who fill their own pockets; he defends 'Holy church' against 'lollers' (Lollards) about whose opinions however he appears to know little.

The Lollards originated as followers of the bible translator John Wyclif (1329-84), whose attacks on the endowments and power of the church attracted followers hard-pressed by war taxation. Wyclif, himself at one

---

[49] Norfolk Records Society vol. XIX Pt. 1; at that time South Creake was in the adjacent Norfolk archdeaconry for which there are no records.

[50] *The Vision of Piers Plowman,* William Langland ed. Burrell (Dent 1945) p. 97

[51] Langland (1945) pp. 125, 131

time an absentee rector and Oxford academic, was a major participant in the contemporary debate as to how Christ's poverty should be reflected in the life of the church and whether the church's corruptions deprived it of its right to what was called 'dominion'; practically, whether therefore its possessions should be forfeit to the Crown in time of national need such as war, or even universally as a matter of principle. This was a debate in which the monks and friars found themselves on opposite sides[52]. The latter owed their existence to the practice of such as St. Francis and St. Dominic for whom Christ-likeness meant living as poor preachers, which their orders had originally practised (but which, as Langland had noted, they had long ceased to do). Wyclif's later criticism of church authority and its sacramental doctrine was part of a wider debate but one which he took to extremes of personal animosity; he eventually came to oppose all forms of religious life. Following his condemnation and the events that followed, debate was stifled: 'criticism was associated with heterodoxy'[53].

In spite of their stated denials, both Wyclif and Langland are thought of as being among the intellectual progenitors of the Peasants' Revolt which took place in the summer of 1381and their ideas and even words appear in the language of its leaders. Though its focus was London and Kent the Revolt affected sixteen counties, mostly in the south and east, including Norfolk. The precipitating cause was the imposition of a poll tax, perceived to be unfair in its terms and whose enforcement was resisted not only by peasants. There had been rumblings for some time – confederacies of villeins – relating mostly to their newly realisable desire to escape their serf status. Issues raised ranged from the radical demand for the creation of an egalitarian society including the abolition of the monarchy to higher wages (artificially held down by statute[54]), the abolition of feudal dues and the curbing of the activities of foreign merchants. John Ball's famous question 'When Adam delve (dug) and Eve span (spun) who was then the gentleman?' in his Blackheath sermon on June 12th became the rallying cry of many of the protesters. One action above all characterised the movement: the destruction of manorial records, the visible evidence of men's status as free or unfree and of rents and ownership. Monasteries were a prime target,

---

[52] *The Religious Orders in England* vol II, David Knowles (Cambridge 1959) p. 61ff.
[53] Pantin (1955) p. 238; see also Knowles (1959) p. 72, 101f. In crossing the boundaries of orthodoxy Wyclif parted with friends among the friars, who ironically were largely responsible for his condemnation, but he was never excommunicated.
[54] Statute of Labourers 1351; shortage of labour meant that men could demand higher wages; the statute was meant to limit wage rises.

but so were the houses of lawyers and members of parliament. The local centre of violence was Norwich and its environs; the first great meeting took place at Moushold heath outside the city a matter of days after John Ball's sermon; in that week mobs roamed where they pleased: on June 15th a Justice of the Peace near Walsingham was pursued in peril of his life so that he boarded a boat and was pursued as far as Burnham; on June 21st a mob destroyed the records of the prestigious Binham priory. Trial records show that disturbances took place in Wighton, Lynn, Snettisham, Heacham, and Rudham as well as in the south and west of the county[55]. Evidently there was systematic encouragement to join the revolt from the London rebels by those sent from village to village on horseback in the name of Geoffrey Litster, a dyer from near North Walsham, who had become the local leader. The disorder allowed scores to be settled against unpopular authorities, both secular and religious. There was much killing on both sides. There were attempts by the some of the insurgents not merely to destroy but to replace charters and establish a new order, but these came to nothing. On the arrival of the 'warlike' bishop of Norwich Henry Despenser at the end of June, its leaders, including Litster, were executed, Despenser having heard his confession, and the insurgents dispersed. Despenser had a mass said in thanksgiving for the ending of the riots. A general amnesty by Parliament to the rioters excluded 287 offenders[56].

Like a strong wind the revolt wrought devastation wherever it blew and was gone. After it manorial lords reimposed their rights over their unfree tenants; in some places there is no evidence of any disruption; the involvement of townspeople and the attacks on foreign merchants suggest economic as much as political motives: but the back of villeinage had been broken, the influence of the religious life weakened. The villagers doubtless heard the voices of 'lollers' and hedge priests as well as of friars, monks and lords. Whomever they believed there was still mass on Sundays the only relief from work in the fields; and there was the harvest to get in.

The loss of population caused by the plague and the consequent dislocation of social life affected everyone. Monasteries suffered loss of numbers. In the absence of sufficient lay monks to serve at mass in monasteries so-called almonry boys from the villages were employed. Creake Abbey was an

---

[55] *The Rising in East Anglia in 1381,* Edgar Powell (Cambridge 1896) p. 26ff., App.II
[56] Ibid.

Augustinian house and would have required a few such boys who would have acquired something of an education in order for them to function.

Good times - the community of the parish (1400-1530)

With the improvement of life chances in the village, a degree of differentiation began to emerge: prosperous tenants financed their land dealings by marketing their surplus agricultural produce, by engaging in cottage industries, by lending money or corn at high rates of interest to their needy neighbours and serving the administration of the manor[57]. The village had a weekly market, from which the Beaufoes had claimed dues since 1275[58]. It was granted a charter by Edward I in 1280 and survived until the seventeenth century. Foldcourses were enclosed for sheep, which would be pastured after harvest to fertilise the stubble. The church continued to provide social glue to the community. Piety directed money towards the church and its life. Wills indicate that work on the building began again in the early part of the 1400s. John Bokenham who died in 1412 left 6s.8d. to

'covering the church', presumably the roof[59], though whether his hopes came to fruition then or later there is no way of knowing.

By this time, the exuberant Decorated style of architecture had given way to a new more austere style subsequently called Perpendicular – from the fact that the large windows are made up of horizontal transoms and vertical mullions with little in the way of flamboyant curved shapes as in the earlier period. Originating during the 1330s, its simpler structure may have been an advantage after the Black Death when many masons died; it later enabled much larger windows which were filled with stained glass. Unique

---

[57] *The Agrarian Problem of the Sixteenth Century*, R.H. Tawney (London 1912) p. 72-87,93

[58] Blomefield (1806) p. 79

[59] Norfolk Archaeology (1983) Vo. 38 p. 244

to England[60], it was a style that dominated until most building stopped with the Reformation. The late flowering of the style was in the later part of the century after 1471 when Edward IV came back from exile in Burgundy bringing the Wars of the Roses to a temporary halt. Because he resolved to 'live of his own' so that taxes were lessened there was money around. Local wills indicate the building of a shrine to the godly king Henry VI[61] (who had been executed on Edward's return in 1471) which also suggests a later date. All this then will have taken place during the sixty-one year incumbency of William Crane, by some accounts a member of a local landed family.

The sacristy and the rood – the figure of Christ crucified in the chancel arch – together with its screen and loft which date from this time hint at a change towards a faith more focussed on Christ's Passion which was now set before the congregation whenever they entered the building. (The present rood was

brought from Colchester in 1982, its predecessor having been torn down during the Reformation as we shall see. Only the staircase and the defaced screen remain of the original). The rood loft was huge and extended from the arch to which it was fixed forward into the nave. Below it was the screen, which still survives, on which was painted pictures of the saints, probably the apostles, and almost certainly, an image of the Virgin Mary. Behind the rood within the chancel arch would have been a Doom, a painting of the Day of Judgement (whose onetime presence is indicated by the removal of the upper part of the hood moulding over the arch)[62].

The great work on the building was the rebuilding of the nave; its long sloping roof[63] was replaced by a two stage slate roof, the upper one ending in a clerestory pierced by windows of the new style; the lower aisle roofs

---

[60] Continental influence ceased during the French wars. Cf. Howard (1936) p. 79

[61] Will of Lawrence Norton 1505 NRO PD612/117. Henry VII sought to promote the cause of his canonization as a means of justifying the legitimacy of his dynasty.

[62] A rare example of a Doom survives in the parish of Wenhaston in Suffolk.

[63] The old roof line can be seen on the east face of the tower.

ended in heavily buttressed outer walls between which were even larger versions of the same four pointed arched windows, thus transforming the building with a flood of light, coloured by stained glass. There was a new window above the chancel arch. Only the exterior walls remained of the older building. The new hammer beamed roof with its choirs of painted angels completed the process.

Of the same period was the Seven Sacrament font its eight sides being completed with a carving of the crucifixion. The 'Hexagonal goblet' pulpit was of the same time, each panel once painted probably with representations of the four Latin Doctors (teachers) of the Church, St, Gregory, St. Ambrose, St. Augustine and St. Jerome; evidently preaching, probably in the form of catechesis, was alive. (A similar pulpit, at the nearby Burnham Norton, on which the paintings remain, gives some idea what it would have looked like.) Representations of the Latin Doctors were very popular.

As there were supporters so there were detractors. In 1429 William Colyn, a skinner of South Creake, on being asked to contribute to the painting of images in church said he would rather give a shilling to their being burnt[64]. Foxe, the martyrologist, wrote of John Beverley, a labourer of South Creake who was sent to Norwich Castle, kept in irons and whipped 'as he had eaten flesh on a fast day'[65]. Guessingly, this was no mere act of inadvertence. Lollardy was not quite dead. Parliament had passed legislation allowing for the execution by burning of heretics in 1401, and though bishop Alnwick of Norwich had been vigorous in their prosecution three men only, not including our South Creake men, were executed out of a total of over a hundred arrested and examined[66].

There were apparently six side altars, in addition of the high altar, an indication that there was a number of chantry priests attached to the church, for a priest had to say his mass each day and an altar could only be used once. Lawrence Norton in 1505 wanted a priest to say a requiem for him for seven years; his father John, who died in 1498, asked for a priest to go on

---

[64] *Norwich Heresy Trials 1428-31*, Camden 4th Series 20 ed. N.P. Tanner (Royal Historical Society 1977) pp.89-91 Colyn then refused the penance of saying prayers before a statue of the Blessed Virgin.
[65] *A History of Norfolk*, R. Mason (1884) p. 222
[66] Mason (1884) p. 221

pilgrimage and to sing thirty masses for his soul[67].

The main function of chantries was the saying of Mass for the dead for which a priest was paid a stipend, but in many places they came to acquire others. Testators latterly came to include a provision in their wills that the chantry priest would 'teach children freely'[68]. With the arrival of printed books from the 1470s onwards primers, lay prayer books, which had long circulated in manuscript, were made available to a larger reading public. Works such as *The Book of Good Manners* were translated and printed by Caxton for the pious lay market. John Whitford's *A Work for Householders,* a manual of practical family religion, went through eight editions between 1530 and 1538; a *Primer* of devotions for use at home or in church went through a staggering seventy eight editions between 1501 and 1538[69]. The ban on English versions of the New Testament had to a large extent been ameliorated by the production of the Carthusian Prior Nicholas Love's translation of the *Meditationes Vitae Christi,* essentially an expanded gospel harmony[70].

Increasingly, during the fifteenth century gilds (see below) also endowed schools. As with so many matters, the record is silent as to what precisely went on in South Creake but it is likely that literacy was the possession of a definite if minority percentage of the folk of the village: the Townshends, the Nortons and the Bolters. As to what was taught in the new books, it was part practical – the seven works of corporal mercy, and part theological: intended to enable readers to shorten their time in purgatory. Purgatory was classically the ante-room of Heaven, but it was sometimes more grimly

---

[67] *Index of Wills proved by Norwich Consistory Court 1330-1550* (Norfolk Record Society Vol. XVI Pt. II)

[68] *English Schools at the Reformation,* A.F. Leach, (London 1896) p. 116; Nicholas Orme (2006) p. 237-8

[69] *English Reformations,* Christopher Haig, (Oxford 1992) p. 26

[70] Duffy (1992) p. 78-9; the Carthusians were a major source of such writings.

described as an outpost of Hell[71]. In any case, the means by which men shortened their time of purgation was by generosity especially when making their wills. The parable of the sheep and the goats and the teaching of the difficulty of a rich man entering the kingdom were well known and taught.

Comparative wealth, independence and literacy made for a greater degree of differentiation. Whereas a manorial community was bound together by duty the new 'parish notables' began to share the values of the gentry and to distance themselves not least by screening themselves from the common folk within the church building[72]; the north aisle screen in St. Mary's may have served such a purpose; it serves no liturgical purpose. Pews, made more necessary when listening to sermons, began to appear. Originally erected as free seats, a charge would sometimes be made for their use thus further differentiating the congregation by income and status[73]. The aristocracy meanwhile often built their own chapels and employed their own chaplains from among the friars,[74] sometimes ignoring the need for permission to do so, sometimes sustaining their piety by books of prayers for private devotion. John Townshend whose yeoman farmer family was to become the biggest landowner in the village and who held two manors and land around Raynham in his last bedridden days was attended by a local friar from the Carmelite House at Burnham Norton[75]. A man of conventional piety, a daily mass attender, John expressed concern if he missed a day and was sufficiently anxious for the state of his soul as to leave considerable sums for masses to be said after his death[76]. Described by a contemporary as 'a mean man of substance' his appears to have been a hard-headed piety, investing where he thought most profitable. In religion, as in other things, human beings are often a self-serving. But there is no doubt as to his anxiety to secure his eternal future. He seems not to have been very different from the more famous Pastons, another Norfolk family, whose numerous letters reveal a spirituality adorning a tough-minded approach to business[77]. His

---

[71] Duffy (1992) p. 343

[72] N.J.G. Pounds (2000) p. 251

[73] ibid. p. 243; pew rents became attached to ownership of a particular property.

[74] The mendicant friars, wandering religious who arrived from Europe in the thirteenth century, were not directly answerable to diocesan authorities and disputed both theologically and pastorally with them: see Pantin (1955) p. 124

[75] *The Townshends and their World*, C.E. Moreton (Cambridge 1992) p. 7; he died in 1466.

[76] Moreton (1992) p. 18; he died in 1493.

[77] *Illustrated Letters of the Paston Family,* ed. Roger Virgoe (Macmillan) 1989)

son Sir Roger Townshend was able to exploit the indebtedness of a Rutland squire, one William Beaufoy and in 1475 acquired his manor in the village for £100[78] (thus breaking a link going back almost to the Conquest). His grandson was equally conventional in more ambiguous times suppressing institutions which had supported his grandfather's faith[79]. Subsequently ennobled the Townshends held their land in the village (and later acquired the patronage of the church) until 1935.

Rose's Manor owned by Calthorp family, whose connections go back to the thirteenth century, was sold in 1535 to the merchant Pepys family; they became not only considerable landowners but also pillars of the church as we shall see. They were related to the diarist Samuel Pepys who used to write of his 'Norfolk cousins'. They in turn sold it in 1605 to Sir Edward Coke of Holkham (in whose family's hands it remains). Of the tenanted land the largest holding was in the hands of the Norton family in 1475, which also combined affluence with piety: four wills between 1451 and 1505 show generosity to the church and to its several gilds[80]. By the sixteenth century the Norton's fortunes had declined while that of the Townshends increased: in 1516 Roger Townshend owned 18,000 sheep; by 1559 the family held a quarter of the land in the village in addition to the demesne lands which they held at nearby Raynham[81].

The community of the parish increasingly manifested itself through the gilds. Popular initiative was to become widespread. Gilds, local religious associations of parishioners, had existed since the tenth century but their growth in popularity in the fourteenth and fifteen centuries was

---

[78] Blomefield (1806) p. 79; Moreton (1992) p. 119

[79] See p. 32

[80] Transcripts of wills of John, Robert, Richard and Lawrence Norton, NRO PD 612/117

[81] Moreton (1992) p. 8; Hesse (1998) p. 88

phenomenal[82]. Kings Lynn had seventy; Great Yarmouth nineteen[83]; little South Creake at various times had seven. They were the gilds of the Resurrection, the Holy Cross, St. Ann, the Holy Rood, St. John, Our Lady and the Holy Trinity[84]. Whatever gilds may have been in large towns and in the city of London rural gilds were predominantly religious associations devoted to the obsequies of the parish church, its maintenance, the corporal works of mercy and to prayer for the souls of the departed in the parish. The light before each gild altar had to be tended on Sundays and feast days of which there were many. Gilds sometimes dominated the life of a parish; in some places they ebbed and flowed; some were exclusive, few embraced the whole village[85]. Their widespread existence suggests a vibrancy of parishes as communities which, contrary to what is often believed, were not priest-dominated; the financial muscle, after all, was elsewhere. Funds, sometimes called 'stores', were administered for the benefit of the church and for the promotion of local charity.

Likewise churchwardens, whose origins are obscure, appear, through the preservation of their accounts from the fourteenth century, as increasingly significant administrators of parishes and were a not always comfortable counterbalance to the clergy. Almost always drawn from the ranks of manorial tenants and farmers rather than the aristocracy and chosen by parishioners[86],they gradually assumed responsibility for the repair of the fabric of the church and probably for extension and rebuilding. The effects of this energy are transparent. In St. Mary's, as elsewhere, the nave was the subject of lay effort; the chancel meanwhile, the rector's responsibility, was neglected. They undertook more routine responsibilities: they administered rents, took charge of moneys left for memorial masses and obits; they bought wax, candles and oil for the church, paid the wages of minor church servants, saw to the repair of service books and bought the expensive new missal, or mass book[87]. Their command of income, which did not include

---

[82] *Gilds in the Medieval Countryside 1350-1558,* Virginia Bainbridge (Woodbridge 1996) p. 6
[83] Duffy (1992) p. 142
[84] Blomefield (1806) p. 84; will of Lawrence Norton 1505 NRO PD 612/117
Probably at no one time were all these gilds in operation; three are mentioned in 1451; five in 1505, not including one, St. Anne, mentioned in 1451.
[85] Bainbridge (1996) p. 13
[86] *The Shaping of a Community,* Beat Kumin (Scolar Press 1996) p. 22ff.
[87] Platt (1981) p. 89; this would have been handwritten by monks. Printed missals appeared around 1500.

the income of gilds and chantries exceeded that of the crown in lay direct taxation[88].

Even parishioners who had no responsibilities and may not have been members of gilds frequently gave or left money in their wills for the fabric and that their souls might be prayed for in perpetuity to lessen their time in purgatory. Theology as well as a good name had its effect upon the life of the church in these better times. The Mass was not merely a remembrance but had intercessory value as being the meeting place of heaven and earth where prayer might be heard; merely hearing Mass was held to be efficacious both for the body and the soul.

 Nevertheless, for ordinary people life was hard even in good times: there would be little work in winter; keeping warm depended upon the vagaries of weather; in summer labour was long and demanding and ill-health meant penury or worse. The order of life was precarious; it could be violent - most men carried a weapon. As the better off peasants accumulated land so the number of landless poor increased. Increasingly, households, not only of the great, employed servants, both domestic and farm, who would be housed on the farm and eat around the farmhouse kitchen table. Their position was relatively secure, for the year, but their condition varied depending on their employer. Something of all of this can be seen in the two sides of human character expressed in the stop heads at the ends of the label over the chancel arch. One may be in an attitude of ecstasy, the other is sceptical. This kind of 'baboonery', as it was called, is not uncommon in medieval churches. Life expectancy was short and while the church was not slow to remind folk of the realities of sin and death and the necessity of preparation for death in order to shorten the pains of purgatory the response was sometimes irreverent. Parish life was marked by both elements: holy days were both sacred and secular, and church ales – fundraising events of the day – produced their own kind of solace.

The cycle of the Church's year with its feasting and fasting were woven into people's lives. Daily attendance at mass in order to see the Elevation of the Host was not uncommon encouraged no doubt by preaching on its alleged

---

[88] Kumin (1996) p. 193

therapeutic effects[89]. Music, mostly the chanting of psalms and canticles but including carols, telling both biblical and legendary stories were a feature of Sunday worship. The clerk, perhaps assisted by choir men, would also sing the mass. Feasts such as Candlemass were marked by outdoor processions, in that case with candles, which, in some places were then taken home to be lit later as a remedy against thunderstorms or in times of sickness or placed in the

hands of the dying. Gilds might perform a dramatic enactment of the biblical story during the procession and prior to the mass. Of seasonal observances the Holy Week ceremonies were the most elaborate. They began with the Palm Sunday procession and the distribution of palms when the Passion gospel was read or sung from the Rood loft at the foot of the Rood whose Lenten veil was removed for the occasion. The Easter Triduum, the three days of the Passion story, began with the Maundy Thursday mass and vigil followed by the Good Friday ceremonies when clergy and laity alike crept on their knees, barefoot, to kiss the cross. At the end of the formal liturgy a Host, consecrated on the Thursday, was laid in the Easter Sepulchre still to be seen on the north side of the chancel and was wrapped in linen cloths. Then, on Easter day the Host was replaced in the hanging pyx above the high altar while the bells were rung and an Easter anthem sung[90] before the first Mass of Easter. The faith, sometimes superstitious and unbiblical, was popular[91].

---

[89] Exaggerated claims as to its effects included that one will not die a sudden death, food tastes better, one does not grow older during mass, or that problems would be solved: Joseph Jungmann *Mass of the Roman Rite* (Burns & Oates 1959) pp. 97-8
[90] Duffy (1992) p. 17-29
[91] Expenditure on devotional objects, such as candles and ornaments, continued to increase significantly until the 1520s and financial support for clergy showed no sign of slackening right until the death of Henry VIII: Kumin (1996) p. 127f.

Several reformations (1530-1660)

All of this was to come to an abrupt end. The Reformation, which affected virtually every country in Europe, had complex causes. It began, effectively, in 1517 when Martin Luther nailed to the door of the church in Wittenburg his 95 theses or complaints against the church. The wider causes which resulted in the taking up of reformist ideas were various: the growth of independent nation states seeking freedom from Rome and able to exercise increasing bureaucratic control over their populaces; a rejection of the absentee power of monastic orders; new scholarship, especially of the Bible, made for questioning if not rejection of the magisterium of the Church and of doctrines such as that of Purgatory of which the Mass had become a focus; and a widely recognised need for reform[92]. The question was what form the reforms would take. Outside London, the reform was mostly a top-down process[93] upon a public largely happy with the exercise of their religion if not with its shortcomings and there were significant incidents of resistance to change which were put down brutally. The so-called Walsingham conspiracy in the spring of 1537 when two lay choristers of Walsingham priory set about organising a revolt against the dissolution and resulted in the execution of eleven men was the most significant but not the only local resistance to the reforms[94]. Over twenty five men were finally involved including the sub-prior Nicholas Mileham and the rector of Waterden, John Punt[95]. The support it received on account of its religious as well as its secular functions tells against the negative view of monasteries widely promulgated; its canons were mostly drawn from the locality including the Creakes[96]. Even where there was conformity the effect upon the life of English parish churches, in every particular, was huge. The change from a Latin to an English liturgy effectively made redundant an

---

[92] Not only reformists but also orthodox churchmen like Reginald Pole, later Archbishop under Mary, and John Colet, Dean of St. Paul's, were proponents of the rooting out of corruption in the church: *Prayer Book and People in Elizabethan and Early Stuart England* Judith Maltby (Cambridge 1998) p. 19; Christopher Haig, (1992) p. 9

[93] In spite of organised and vigorous anti-Catholic preaching from 1530 onwards, Protestantism remained the religion of a minority until the reign of Queen Elizabeth.

[94] *The Walsingham Conspiracy of 1537*, C.E. Moreton (Bulletin of the Institute of Historical Research vol. 63 1990) p. 38; other risings were in Fincham and Buckenham the previous year.

[95] Moreton (1990) p. 30-32

[96] Ibid. p. 40

entire musical tradition[97]. The abolition of almost all holy days as well as the emptying of the church of it is colour and light – statues were removed and paintings whitewashed – were even more powerful reasons why the changes were received sullenly, if obediently, and sometimes with rebellion. The disturbances of 1549 convulsed twenty three counties[98] and while motives were mixed and not all of them were connected with the defence of the old religion - Jack Kett's rebellion in Norwich seems to have had economic causes – ambiguities of attitude reveal themselves even among those who sided with the reformers. Thus the younger Sir Roger Townshend, apparently a pious catholic like his grandfather in his early days[99] , though he became a commissioner for the dissolution and stood to benefit considerably from the dissolution, argued for the sparing of some, sympathised with the Catholic Princess Mary and made no attempt to resist the 1549 rebels. A tendency to conform, ambition and fear of consequences and a desire not to lose what spoils others would have taken in any case doubtless moved some men. As for the institutions themselves, with few exceptions, most lacked sufficient fervour to resist[100]. Even Walsingham's demise was accepted (and prepared for) by its obsequious Prior Vowell.

As far as St. Mary's was concerned the process began earlier. So-called 'abused' images of the saints, before which a candle was lit and which were the focus of devotion and were thought to be superstitious, were the subject of criticism by influential preachers even before the breach with Rome in 1534; by 1536 government Injunctions condemned their use and those of 1538 forbade them. Thus, while there were too many lights in the church for all to be named in Lawrence Norton's will of 1505 when John Norton died in 1545 he bequeathed his soul to Almighty God 'through the intercession of our Blessed Lady Virgin', left money for tithes and the repair of the church, but made no mention of lights or gilds[101]. They had clearly gone.

---

[97] The Ranworth Antiphoner (p.20) is an indication of what was lost.

[98] Christopher Haig (1992) p. 175

[99] *The Townshends and their World,* C.D. Moreton (Cambridge 1992) pp. 35-6; Sir Roger's early notebooks were often inscribed 'IHS' or 'Maria'.

[100] Knowles (1959) vol. III p/ 462ff; the Franciscan Observants and the Carthusians were the most notable resisters; the Augustinian canons the most pliable..

[101] NRO/ANF will register Liber 11 (Manclerke), fo. 219. The will of Alice Norton, widow of Richard who died in 1549, the first year of Edward VI, makes no mention even of the Virgin Mary.

The surrender by Castle Acre Priory of all its property including the patronage of St. Mary's church took place on November 22nd 1537[102]. The legal formalities were not complete for another twelve months but the association which had lasted nearly four hundred years was at an end; the rights were given to Thomas, duke of Norfolk. The last prior, Thomas Malling, was apparently thought good enough to be in the running for a bishopric but much larger forces were at work than individual merit. The smaller houses, such as Coxford and Hempton, were suppressed in 1536, the larger, such as Walsingham and Binham, in 1539. (Creake Abbey, having been 'piteously burnt' in 1483, was in the process of rebuilding following a handsome gift from the king and various gifts by will, escaped the dissolution only by having ended its existence thirty three years earlier when all of its members died of 'the sweating sickness'[103])

Finally, on the death of Henry VIII the 1547 Injunctions of his son Edward VI required the removal of roods and the huge lofts on which they stood, statues, stained glass, bells and stone altars; the font was defaced (as can still be seen here), the vestments and church plate were taken away and sold.

Wall paintings were removed or whitewashed over; those on the screen and pulpit were scraped off (literally 'defaced'). Saints' days with their attendant holidays were, most of them, abolished and processions became illegal. In 1549 a new prayer book in English was introduced and the elaborate Holy Week ceremonies were, all of them, forbidden. All the trappings of the old religion were now absent. The task of handing over the offending articles to the Commissioners fell to the churchwardens, William Wheatley and Thomas Pepys, which they performed in 1552[104]. They gave up four complete sets of vestments, black,

---

[102] Page (1906) p. 358

[103] A.L.Bedingfield (1966) p. xxi

[104] *Inventory of Norfolk Church Goods 1552* H.S. Walters, (Norfolk Archaeology vol. XXVI) p. 270

purple, white and red in velvet and damask, two copes, two chalices and patens, a two-manual organ and a ring of five bells, leaving a single bell to call people to worship. The parish had been well provided for. Whether they hid anything as many did (or bought it themselves rather than see it go out of the parish) is not known. Nor was it merely the vesture and furnishings which went. The chancel, long the place for the celebration of the Eucharist, effectively became redundant. (Restored to use in the early seventeenth century until the Commonwealth not until the arrival of robed choirs four hundred years later was a role found for it now again largely lost.)

Meanwhile the abolition of the gilds destroyed a means of local corporate charity as will have been the case with the suppression of chantries. (The Reformation, famed for promoting education, appears initially to have dislocated it by removing a major source of funding)[105].

Ironically, the year after the wardens handed over the church's goods the weakling and very determinedly Protestant Edward VI died. Mary, daughter of Henry VIII's first wife Catherine of Aragon and a Catholic, became Queen. She immediately set about restoring the old religion. Her new Archbishop, Cardinal Pole, instructed parishes to put back their stone altars, repair their rood screens and place once again the figure of Christ crucified, the rood, above the altar; to say the Mass again instead of the recently approved 1552 Book of Common Prayer from which all prayers for the dead had been removed. Vestments and church plate were to be bought; and Mary ordered that, where it could be done, confiscated plate and vestments be restored to the parishes[106]. It was a huge job but gradually it was done. At South Creake they may have got their vestments back but they also lost their vicar. Thomas Leman, appointed in 1540, who had married in the church three years previously as the new religion allowed and who had also signed the document of confiscation, was sent packing[107]. Thomas Markham, the new priest, appointed by the new patron, the Duke of Norfolk, was doubtless celibate. In most places people conformed willingly and many things, from altar stones to vestments, came out of hiding and were put back in Church. Processions and mystery plays resumed; traditions like the Plough Monday

---

[105] Leach (1896) p. 78
[106] Haig, (1992) p. 209
[107] *Married Clergy and Pensioned Religious in Norwich diocese 1555,* G. Baskerville (English Historical Review 1933) p. 43ff.

collections in January were put to use to restore neglected and damaged buildings[108].

Had there been time the old religion would probably have been restored in its fullness though church land once sold could never be recovered (and Pole never tried to do so). People who left money to the church in their wills in return for prayers were less likely to do so now[109]. Another reversal might take place. As it did.

In 1558 Mary died, probably of stomach cancer, and in her place her younger half sister, daughter of Anne Boleyn, the first Queen Elizabeth, was crowned. Elizabeth reigned for forty four years time enough to settle the parish church to a diet of the Book of Common Prayer said in a plain building without any adornment. It took a little time. Bishop Redman's Visitation of the parish in 1597 noted that the table of the Ten Commandments had not yet been provided – to be placed on the chancel wall – nor the Queen's articles provided as required and that the vicar, John Lynsey, did not preach monthly as he was supposed[110]. Yet even from the outset the Reformers, especially those who had returned from exile under Mary, had learned from the previous reversal. Public bonfires of images and books and the persistence of Episcopal visitors in seeking out any concealed objects[111] meant that there was no going back.

The bureaucratic tendency of the Tudor state in local matters, which had begun under Henry VIII, manifested itself in other ways again using the parish as the instrument of its policies. The keeping of parish registers,

---

[108] Haig (1992) p. 212-3

[109] However, in the diocese of Chichester bequests for masses had, by 1557 reached levels rarely surpassed previously, while bequests to the poor were at unprecedented levels: N.J.G Pounds (2000) p. 271

[110] *Bishop Redman's Visitation 1597,* Norfolk Record Society Vol. XVIII (1946).

[111] Duffy (1992) p. 569ff

adequate parish chests and procedures for election of parochial office holders were all requirements added to existing responsibilities over the period. Churchwardens were now required under Elizabeth to fine absentees from Church[112]. Parish responsibilities were extended to the repair of roads and bridges, the control of vermin and the support of the poor. The Elizabethan Poor Law placed responsibility for the raising of funds and finding apprenticeships and employment for the able-bodied on churchwardens[113] replacing the admittedly patchy provision by gilds. Overseers of the Poor were appointed to every parish by the vestry who were subject to the county magistrates. And to pay for these increasing activities compulsory church rates came to be imposed to cover anything from church repairs to the administration of local gaols and the care of maimed soldiers. Increasingly, particularly in towns these burdens were shared with select vestries, regular meetings of representative parishioners, rather than the formal annual gathering. The community of the parish had survived the first two reformations.

The so-called Elizabethan Settlement was not always easy to maintain. On the one hand there were closet Catholics, 'church papists', like Fermor Pepys, one of the patrons of the parish, who went to church in obedience to the law while his family went off to mass[114], as well as recusants – those Catholics who refused to go to church at all and who were prosecuted for it (which last category included yet another Roger Townshend, son and namesake of the despoiler of Walsingham)[115]. The gentry could most readily evade the law though there were some peasant folk who paid the fine and refused give up the old religion. On the other there were those who came to be called Puritans who thought that the process of reform had not gone far enough and who wished the church rid of its bishops and prayer book confining the service to preaching which was, on this view, its only purpose. Somewhere in the middle were those who came to love and revere the prayer book. Elizabeth over her long reign held the line, sometimes with difficulty, though, in her preference for the retention of such objects as crucifixes and altars, she had to give way[116]. Both effectively disappeared

[112] Kumin (1996) p. 243ff

[113] Kumin (1996) p. 248; *Acts for the Relief of the Poor 1597 and 1601*

[114] Pepys' wife, Frances, was prosecuted in 1584 for hearing mass said by a Roman Catholic priest: Norfolk Archeology XXXII (1961)) p. 44; the priest, Montford Scott, was hanged, drawn and quartered: Mason (1884) p. 577

[115] Mason (1884) p.570; see also page 32

[116] *Altars Restored*, Kenneth Fincham & Nicholas Tyacke (OUP 2007) p. 37

the latter to be replaced by a table set half way down the chancel longways around which the congregation sat or knelt.

Elizabeth's reign was not a golden age so far as church buildings were concerned. It was described at the time as a period of fifty year neglect. The removal of internal decoration was central to the Puritan project; the dilapidation of buildings was an almost inevitable consequence. The argument was not merely about externals. The essence of the Puritan argument was that the communion was not a means of grace; nor was preaching on which they laid so much emphasis: for only the chosen, the elect, were saved and the fate of all, saved and unsaved, had been determined already. It was a grim creed. As for the clergy, there was constant complaint that incompetent persons occupied the pulpit[117]; shortage of clergy was a major cause.

By the time James I, son of Mary Queen of Scots, acceded to the throne there were the beginnings of a reaction, first in print, and then upon the interiors of cathedrals and parish churches. After 1625, the new King, Charles I began to encourage a greater concern for the beautification of buildings. Bishops Laud, Neile and Wren, the first two of whom became archbishops, began to insist on the return of altars, the use of copes at the communion, the use of ceremonial and, through their visitations, the restoration of churches[118]. They halted the practice of commerce in church and encouraged, for the first time for many years, the building of new churches. In Norwich diocese, of which Wren was bishop for a time,

---

[117] A Russell, *The Country Parson* (SPCK 1992) p. 56

[118] In the Norwich diocese, churches responded so that they shone 'among us in the primitive splendour, to the great good liking of all sober Christians': Fincham & Tyacke (2007) p. 168. The expression 'the beauty of holiness' became a catch phrase to describe the work of the movement. ibid p. 220

there was both enthusiastic conformity as well as some resistance to change which focussed on the new regulations about receiving communion at the altar rail[119] rather than in their seats in the nave, which Wren enforced across the diocese from 1636. South Creake may well have acquired a new altar surrounded by rails at this time. However, when King Charles, who had not called a Parliament since 1629, had to do so in 1640 in order to secure funds for the war with Scotland, the Puritan majority took its opportunity. Apart from reducing the King's legal powers and those of the Archbishop, Parliament instructed the destruction of altars and their rails[120], the levelling of chancels and the removal of all images, including crucifixes. An officially inspired propaganda campaign was launched for the abolition of bishops and all set forms of prayer 'root and branch'[121] with a view to carrying the Reformation again to what they regarded as its logical conclusion. The opposition of the Puritan rump in Parliament to both King and Church resulted in the English Civil War at the end of which in 1649 Charles (a statue of whom is to be found in South Creake church) was executed. The celebration of festivals such as Christmas was made illegal, pubs were closed; whatever ornaments had survived the Edwardine Reformation were, in parts of East Anglia, to be 'broken down' at the hand of William Dowsing, commissioned by the Roundhead Parliament of Lord Protector Cromwell in 1643. (His records show how much had been retained from the previous century in spite of the work of Elizabeth's Commissioners.) Thus, the violence of the sixteenth century rumbled on for more than a hundred years afterwards – a third 'reformation'. Some say that the angels in the roof at St. Mary's suffered from Roundhead soldiers using them as target practice; the damage is as likely to have been caused by the attempts to rid the church of jackdaws and sparrows[122] but the story epitomises the attitude of Cromwell's army to church buildings[123]. In any case, it was the first war since before the Conquest directly to affect the lives of ordinary people, dividing families and laying waste villages and countryside.

Thomas Lynge had been vicar of the parish since 1617, a Suffolk man from the village of Kentford. He had only just been ordained and he served

---

[119] Fincham & Tyacke (2007) p. 214-217

[120] Some were hidden and returned at the restoration: ibid. p. 277

[121] The petitions to remove episcopacy were centrally organised whereas the counter-petitions show all the marks of local initiative: Maltby (1998) p. 86 & 97

[122] See *South Creake Churchwardens Accounts 1667-1790*, Norfolk Records Office.

[123] See, for instance *Hard Measures,* Joseph Hall (1808). Hall was bishop of Norwich from 1641-1656 who observed the vandalising of the cathedral.

throughout the reign of Charles and the Commonwealth remaining in post until he died in 1657 the year before Cromwell's death. His observance of the rites of the Book of Common Prayer would have had to have been clandestine; officially it had been replaced by the Directory of Worship issued in 1645 though this book was scarcely bought by anyone certainly in Norfolk. Funerals were particularly offensive to those who called themselves 'the godly'[124] because they implied that anyone might be 'asleep in the Lord'.

The Restoration – dissent, new knowledge and enclosure (1660-1820)

Thomas Howlet, Lynge's successor, saw the restoration in and died in post. With the early resignation of Cromwell's son Richard in 1660, the old king's son, a second Charles, was brought to England from continental exile and enthroned. The Book of Common Prayer was brought back into use in 1662, much as Queen Elizabeth had reintroduced it, though after some argument; bishops were consecrated and clergy ordained; churches were restored to use. The task was huge: Norwich cathedral was in ruins; many parish churches were in a poor state; but grass roots support for the reinstatement of railed altars and the weekly celebration of the Eucharist, was encouraged, indeed exhorted by bishops[125]. A sense of reverence and order in worship was to be allowed to return. In fact, some things remained much the same; some things changed. In St. Mary's the Holy Communion was celebrated only at Christmas, Palm Sunday, Easter, Low Sunday and Whitsunday[126] and visitation articles of the time indicate that this was the expected pattern. The bells and church clock were repaired, the dial of the latter repainted; various bits of glazing were done; and some building repairs. They seemed to have trouble with birds: rooks, jackdaws and

---

[124] Maltby (1998) p. 60-1

[125] William Lloyd, bishop of Norwich, from 1685 -1691 urged frequent and serious preparation for 'the lords supper': Fincham & Tyacke (2007) p. 330

[126] *South Creake Churchwarden's Accounts (as above)*

sparrows by the dozen. In 1682, the parish also paid for 'stopping ye staging holes in ye steeple'[127].

The pastoral ministry may have left something to be desired. Apart from introducing English as the language in which the registers were kept, Howlet neglected their keeping, as did his successor Edmund Turner. John Cleaver, who was vicar for forty-one years, died in post; he likewise left huge gaps in the records. Nevertheless, he at least was not an absentee; a note in the register describes him as 'honest old John Cleaver'. The church was the foremost institution in the village: the parish's affairs were conducted by the vicar, the churchwardens and the vestry. The church both ordered and replicated the social relations in the parish. Thus, for instance, pews were allocated according to the social standing of parishioners and rents charged, removing the poor and landless to the back of the church[128]. Outside church, the vestry chose the churchwardens and overseers of the poor - the latter were technically appointed by the county magistrates, and were responsible for the collection of the poor rate and administration of the poor law. The poor rate was not popular and means were continually being sought to reduce it: only those who could prove that they were legally settled in the community could claim it; those who could not might be removed to their previous parish by an order obtained from the justice (by which means the parish was able to send Thomas Webb and his wife to Great Bircham just as the parish of Wighton had sent James and Amy Oliver back to South Creake)[129] ; parishes would indenture orphans as apprentices sometimes in other parishes; they issued bastardy orders against the putative fathers of illegitimate children who would be made to sign a bastardy bond which would be forfeit if the mother or child became a charge on the parish; those found to be mentally ill were sent at a charge on the parish to the county lunatic asylum in Norwich. Additionally sums were paid to those in need as payment for work done or sometimes for the purchase of clothes or even food[130]. As an unpaid office, that of overseer was not much sought after and could be carried out compassionately or heartlessly. Accounts do not reveal those to whom help was refused.

Churchwardens also administered charitable funds intended for the benefit of the village. Thus, in 1640 Dorothy Woodhouse had left 20s. from

---

[127] ibid.

[128] Pound (2000) p. 473-4

[129] NRO PD 553/66; PD 34/36

[130] *The Poor Law in Norfolk 1700-1850*, J. Crowley and A. Reid (Ely 1983) p. 6ff.

property to the minister, on condition that he preached two sermons a year, the remainder to be distributed to the poor. In 1668 Isaac Lane left £100 for the building of what became known as the Town House to provide accommodation for four poor families also paying for the building of a school (which however subsequently fell down for want of repairs)[131]. In 1732, his daughter Elizabeth Pell left £100 for the poor of South Creake. John Ward had left an annuity of 40s. in 1700 and in 1787 Samuel Cousley had left the interest on £50[132]. People gave or bequeathed money to the poor, no longer to secure their swift passage through Purgatory, but instead money was given for charitable causes in acknowledgement of biblical exhortations. Since salvation was achieved by means of the Word of God preaching and literacy were of the essence[133].

The Restoration brought an end to eighteen years of censorship and restriction with the inevitable reaction: in London the court of Charles II encouraged sexual licence and bawdy entertainment. Doubtless that little affected South Creake, but the lurch back again with the accession of the Calvinist William and Mary in 1688 undoubtedly did. William, married to James II's sister, was prince of Orange and the 'Glorious Revolution' was in fact an invasion. He arrived with 14,000 soldiers to claim the throne which would enable him the better to wage war with the Catholic French.

The king warned his subjects that God might withdraw his gracious favour from the kingdom were profanity and immorality not curbed. Every parish priest had to see to it that the churchwardens presented to the ecclesiastical courts all those guilty of adultery and fornication in the parish[134]. The consistory courts had survived the Reformation and the Commonwealth.

---

[131] *White's Gazetteer and Directory of Norfolk* 1836. p. 624
[132] Ibid.
[133] *Lay People and Religion in the Early Eighteenth Century,* W.M. Jacob (Cambridge 1996) p.156, 162
[134] Jacob (1996) p. 124f

The court in Norwich was busier in 1744 than it had been in 1507. Since the court had no power to compel attendance and no penal sanctions it could enforce, its use can only have been the result of public support. Adulterers and fornicators were made to do public penance[135]: thus, on April 11th 1731 Mary Barker of North Creake stood in the aisle of the church, as required by the court, for the duration of the service 'cloathed in a white sheet with a white wand in her hand, a paper pinned to her breast' setting out her fault (and the name of her co-fornicator) and then, at the end of the service made an act of penitence on her knees before the congregation[136]. Slanderers were fined, neighbour disputes which were 'contrary to the rules of Christian charity' were dealt with by penance also in church (but on a weekday) and wills were proved. Partly because it was cheaper, people preferred church justice to that of the common law. Samuel Cousley, whose generosity we have noticed, appeared before the court in 1744 while still a bachelor for an act of fornication but was allowed his penance to be commuted to a money payment[137]; this became a widespread practice amongst those who could afford it. The going rate was two guineas to be given to charity. Only as the century passed did the use of the court wane as Dissenters refused to attend and issues of morality were somewhat privatised; after about 1780, illegitimacy rates began to rise dramatically (as did the number of pregnant brides) [138]. They did not fall until the 1870s, perhaps the belated result of Victorian morality

The Church of England was still the established church but it was no longer the national church, nor was it without its critics in Parliament as well as outside. Charitable giving was regarded by some parliamentarians as a means of bolstering it up and made it more difficult by the Mortmain Act of 1736. This invalidated charitable dispositions of land in wills unless they were made in the last year of the testator's life. Such giving noticeably diminished as a result though the act was badly drafted and easily circumvented.

Some of the disputants about the character of the Church, the Dissenters, unable to stomach the restored Prayer Book had been deprived. The

---

[135] Two thirds of the cases heard in Norwich Consistory Court in the 1740s were for fornication or adultery: Jacob (1996) p. 142

[136] NRO/DN/CON/86/1

[137] Ibid.

[138] *The Population of Victorian and Edwardian Norfolk,* Alan Armstrong (2000) p. 109f.

Toleration Act of 1689 had freed them from the duty of worship in the parish church. These Non-Conformists thus became a permanent separate feature of the landscape. Initially, prevented by law from preaching in towns and cities, Dissenting ministers were reduced to setting up chapels outside them, which they did; because they functioned without parish boundaries and drew people from a distance, they may have contributed to the breakup of the self-identification of parishes as religious communities[139]. Few in numbers – some 6% of the population in the early years of the century – their influence was disproportionate; parliamentary support for the new pluralism threatened the Anglican monopoly. On the other side, dissent was feared as a source of radicalism particularly during the Napoleonic wars.

The process of separation was gradual. Chapel building did not begin in earnest until the 1770s and many people until then remained church-goers as well as attending meeting houses; this was sometimes accepted, sometimes not: 'occasional conformity', attendance at church by dissenters (and Roman Catholics) saved them from disqualification for public office which otherwise applied to them, something which caused huge dissension in Parliament. The first chapel in South Creake was built in 1779 on the initiative of Ann and Martha Glover, members of a local farming family – their cousin Philip was tenant of Manor Farm. Their declared reason for acting was the fact that the incumbent of the time, the Revd. William Fisher, was an absentee and that Sunday services were held 'only once a week or fortnight'. The parish was, it was later said, 'a very destitute place spiritually'. The two ladies ran the services themselves and, in course of time, the work was handed over to the Baptists. After a number of years it declined and closed. It re-opened in 1840, following the establishment in 1833 of South Creake as a Home Mission

---

[139] *Rural Society and the Anglican Clergy 1815-1914,* Robert Lee (Boydell 2006) p. 59f

Station by the Congregational Church[140]. It met first of all in a converted dwelling house and appears to have acquired the chapel, (which now belongs to a musical trust) in 1844.

There were other sources of potential weakness. Not only did Protestants of various kinds break away; there were others, high churchmen who, when James II, a Roman Catholic, succeeded his brother Charles and then abdicated under pressure, refused to swear allegiance to the new monarchs, William and Mary,; among them was the bishop, William Lloyd. These, non-Jurors, many of them scholarly, were another loss to the Church when they were deprived. This mattered quite a lot. The church lives by its devotion, but it also lives by its ability to engage with the world. And the world was changing. The so-called Enlightenment had come. Scholars were looking at the world, law, government, the natural order, the stars in the heavens, without reference to religion and some had come to sceptical conclusions. Religion, it was argued even within the church, did not need revelation; its essence was reason and harmony with nature[141]. It was a cloud no bigger than a man's hand; the harmonious character of nature was to be exploded by Darwin and in any case religion understood as explanation was insufficient. Explanations do not drive conduct. It was a time when scholarly as well as devoted churchmen were needed. Fortunately, some Christians felt able to engage, one of them being a vicar of South Creake. He was the Revd. Samuel Vince M.A., F.R.S., vicar from 1786 until 1821, whose day job was that of Plumian Professor of Astronomy and Experimental Philosophy in the University of Cambridge. Vince was also Archdeacon of Bedford and Rector of Kirkley in Suffolk, but his studies took him away from any ecclesiastical tasks and the parish was cared for by a succession of curates, the last of whom, Thomas Scrimshire, succeeded him on his death. Vince had been a bricklayer's son but was sent to school and then to Caius College Cambridge by a clergyman who saw him reading one day and lent him some books. His interests were mathematical but he took time to write a refutation of the arguments of the sceptical Scottish philosopher, David Hume[142]. He typified the absenteeism

---

[140] Norfolk Records Office FC23/1

[141] E.g. *Christianity not mysterious* by John Toland (1696) ; *Christianity as old as the Creation* by Matthew Tindal (1730)

[142] *The Credibility of Christianity Vindicated, in Answer to Mr. Hume's Objections; in Two Discourses* preached before the University of Cambridge, the Rev. S. Vince (1798)

which affected half the parishes in Norfolk, though his curates appear to have been assiduous, as we shall see.

Vince's ministry, or rather that of his various curates, encompassed a major European transformation, that effected by the French Revolution and the Napoleonic wars which followed. The Revolution was at first received with joy. Not only Frenchmen but some Englishmen, such as the pamphleteer John Thelwall, also chose to call themselves Jacobins and to defend, even the horrors of the terror because of the radical egalitarianism that it stood for[143]. The rise of pamphleteering and of radical protest was epitomised by *The Rights of Man,* written by Thetford born Thomas Paine and published in 1791, which was printed in huge numbers and distributed across the land. Paine was no socialist: he defended the rights of manufacturers and traders; he reserved his hostility for the hereditary principle. Thereafter, until their banning in 1794, meetings of radicals were organised by imitation rather than directive, the main thrust of which was against Church and King in favour of universal suffrage under a republic. In religion many of its leaders were atheist or Deist – believers in a divine first cause but excluding the Christian revelation. Pitt's government, in fear, added to the number of capital offences by banning meetings of more than 50 and incitement to hatred of the King, the Constitution or government[144].

One of the earliest societies to be formed in response to the revolution was the so-called Norwich Revolution Society formed as early as 1789. One of its founders, the Revd. Mark Wilks, a Baptist minister made, so bold as to assert that 'Jesus Christ was a revolutionist', adding that the Revolution was of God[145]. Dissent in Norwich had long been strong. As the revolution over the water became more violent the society lost its merchant membership and became more radical; its disbandment with the arrest of its secretary Isaac Saint was nevertheless followed by the creation in 1795 of the more moderate Norwich Patriotic Society which argued for parliamentary reform. T.W. Coke of Holkham, owner of Rose's Manor and famous as an agricultural innovator and liberal supporter, was a subscriber to its short-lived periodical *The Cabinet*[146]. The movement might have been about ideas and in part it was, but in 1795 a new instructor among the masses appeared, namely want. The exceptionally hard winter of 1794-5 drove wheat prices to

---

[143] *The Making of the English Working Class,* E.P. Thompson (Penguin 1968) p. 200
[144] Thompson (1968) p.159
[145] *Norwich since 1550,* ed. C. Rawcliffe and P. Wilson (Continuum 2004) p. 182
[146] Thompson (1968) p. 156

astronomical levels. In 'Jacobin' Norwich, according to John Thelwall, 25,000 workers were claiming relief. In Wells there were riots as a great many women, supported by some men, prevented the loading of flour onto ships destined for the London market[147]; the mob was only dispersed by the bayonets of the militia. The Norwich society had numerous branches and it was reported that there were 'affiliated societies in every town and almost every village in Norfolk'[148]. The villagers of South Creake certainly suffered from the price of wheat and may have seen the literature which included comment on its causes. The protest, though widespread, lacked cohesion and by 1797 increasing fears of invasion united more of the public behind a government which had combined draconian legislation with the use of spies and agent provocateurs to disarm the considerable protest which talk of revolution and change had spawned. Brothercross Hundred was one of many from which were recruited Yeomanry Cavalry under the command of William Hoste Esq. as a defence against a French invasion[149].

Hunger undoubtedly affected civil order; war harmed commerce and created labour shortages; radical ideas influenced the public mood, but arguably the biggest long term influence on the village, as on the countryside as a whole, was the loss to villagers of their common rights through what was called Enclosure. Hitherto, the ancient strip system of farming still largely obtained hereabouts, villagers 'working within earshot of each other, talking as they worked'; the landscape was open, the common grazed, its fruits gathered. Under the system, field marks had to be periodically named, a process in which the whole parish took part; the proportion of arable and pasture had to be managed by twice yearly field orders (which had to be agreed and nailed to the door of the parish church); after the harvest the fields were opened up to gleaners and as stubble for the herds, and then for the sheep[150]; the common was not only for grazing but for fish, hares, nuts, turf, fowling, peat, and firewood among other things. It is estimated that, even by the early eighteenth century, land over which commoners had rights, including small landowners, made up a half the acreage of the county, over a quarter of the country as a whole[151]; so the effects of the loss of amenity were huge. The system was held to be inefficient, not allowing

---

[147] Mason (1884) p. 479

[148] Thompson (1968) p. 131; *The Jacobin City,* C.B. Jewson (Blackie 1975) p. 38-9

[149] Mason (1884) p. 460-1

[150] *Commoners: Common Right, Enclosure and Social Change in England, 1700-1820,* J. M. Neeson (Cambridge 1993) p. 3ff.

[151] Ibid. p. 61;

the development of modern farming methods with crop rotation or the improvement of pasture. The enclosure process had begun before Elizabeth but had been piecemeal and slow; encroachment and the buying up of land had taken place over a longer period. 'Closes' would be created for particular purposes – orchards or for livestock – sometimes the lord of the manor or free tenants bought up their neighbours; some fenced 'waste' – uncultivated land including woodland and fenland but which was used for rough grazing and fuel. The Townshend family in particular had hugely increased its holding in the village in the sixteenth century. A prolonged legal action in chancery by them to secure enclosure had taken place in the early 1600s[152].

The pace of enclosure had increased during the eighteenth century by the device of petitioning Parliament to pass private legislation. Parliamentary enclosure enabled the appointment of commissioners, who would hear claims of entitlement to land in the parish and, where there were objections, decide upon them, finally making an award of land to each claimant. Against their award there was no appeal. Thus, in the mid eighteenth century 219 parishioners petitioned Captain Townshend M.P. begging him not to support the projected inclosure [sic] of the commons'[153]. Arthur Young, the agriculturist, recorded that there were still 1000 acres of common in the village in 1804[154]. As prices rose with the Napoleonic blockade T.W. Coke of Holkham secured a number of enclosure acts and bought up any land which he could, often above the market price[155], which he continued up to his death in 1842[156]. North Creake was enclosed in 1809, Great and Little Walsingham in 1812, Wells in 1813; Burnham Deepdale, Burnham Norton and Burnham Overy were enclosed in 1825, and Sculthorpe in 1829. Whereas previously villagers had access to larger pasture, the small pieces of land awarded to them, even if they could afford to fence them, were often too small to be of much use. Landless cottagers most often lost all claim. Enclosure finally came to South Creake in 1859.

Coke was a godly man. He believed that he had been placed by Providence where he was and his philanthropy extended to the provision of decent conditions of tenure for his tenants of housing for his labourers. His

---

[152] Norfolk Records Office BT/T 15/1 1-14

[153] NRO/BL/T 13/56

[154] *General View of the Agriculture of Norfolk,* Arthur Young (1804) p. 388

[155] *Coke of Norfolk,* R.A.C. Parker (Oxford 1975) p. 96

[156] Parker (1975) p. 84-88

proselytising efforts in the improvement of farming became famous (and he was awarded the Earldom of Leicester in 1837 for his pains.). He was also a Whig and a supporter of radical reform[157]. Whether the landless benefitted from his efforts is less sure; their condition 'did not occupy the attention of the Cokes and their advisers until the discontent of the labourers obtruded itself in the 1830s'[158].

Enclosure brought to an end not only a system of agriculture, but an interdependent way of life in which landless cottagers could rely partly on themselves rather than completely on wages or poor relief. The independence of the peasantry with its small cultivated plots and grazing on common pasture and waste was extinguished and replaced by 'a landless rural proletariat', agricultural labourers; indeed as contemporary accounts show, one of its declared purposes was to create a biddable, dependant labouring class[159]. And while tenant farmers had been accustomed to house and feed their servants, who would include stockmen, shepherds and labourers, within their own premises, it was cheaper to pay them a wage and let them go when there was no work to be done[160]. The purpose, that of increasing productivity in order to feed a fast rising mostly urban population was manifestly achieved, and some labourers for the first time secured a regular income; land was set aside for recreation and the purchase of coals, but the increased casualisation of labour brought hardship and even starvation in winter and when harvests were poor. It broke up families and contributed to the rise in illegitimacy. It was permanently to alter the relationship between landowners and labourers in the countryside. Into this process strode the new vicar, Henry Goggs.

Gentrification, reform and education (1821-1905)

Goggs was a local man, whose family owned the water mill at Hempton. He was a hunting parson, a stock caricature figure of the day who, according to a local story, went straight from church on a Sunday to mount his horse at the churchyard wall to go to the hunt, throwing off his surplice as he did so. But his interest in the church building was equal to his passion for hunting.

---

[157] Thompson (1968) p. 156

[158] Parker (1975) p. 165

[159] Neeson (1993) p. 21ff; proposals for compensation of commoners were refused by Parliament: ibid. p.50.

[160] William Cobbett *Political Register* Oct 20th 1825 cited in *Captain Swing,* E.J. Hobsbawm and George Rudé (Penguin 1973) p. 25

He collected as many of the fragments of stained glass as he could and repositioned them in the north aisle, releading the other windows. He had the medieval roof replaced – paid for by the Townshends - with one that was more utilitarian than beautiful and had it releaded. The old roof had been long neglected by his predecessors and was past saving. He provided a new clock for the tower, reseated the church, put in two coke stoves for heating and replaced the churchyard fence with a wall. He had the ring of five bells recast and placed in the sixteenth century bell frame.

Pastorally, however, his ministry was marked by controversy. It was a time when acrimony between parish churches and non-conformist chapels was intensifying. He controlled the churchyard and could prevent dissenting ministers from taking burials there even of their own people. Moreover, even before the 1859 enclosure, its effects in neighbouring villages were already felt. The peasantry had been excluded from access to common land, sometimes even their cottages, built on the waste, had been pulled down. Thus as agricultural wages fell after soldiers returned from war, this affected everyone: some families starved, many men poached, the punishment for which was transportation. Yet others resorted to open and then covert protest against low wages, against unemployment, against poor law rates and for a reduction in tithes. Covert acts took the form of fire raising and animal maiming for which men might be transported or hanged if caught. Beerhouses which, unlike the pubs, were not frequented by the respectable were the meeting places for the 'sullen poor' where plans might be hatched and were thus treated with suspicion. William Shackcloth's beerhouse in the village may have been one such[161].

The so-called Swing Riots of 1830 marked the change in incendiarism from being a sporadic phenomenon to being something of a coordinated movement[162]. 'Captain Swing' was the name by which many threatening

---

[161] Hobsbawm and Rudé (1973) p 40; *White's Gazetteer* 1836 p. 629

[162] The Lucifer match became widely available only in 1830. That year there were 28 fires in Norfolk, in the following two years there were 53 and 52 respectively: *By a*

letters sent to landowners were signed, a pseudonym probably referring to the flail or swinging stick used in manual threshing. The effects of the poor harvests of 1828-9, the hard winter which followed and the growing use of threshing machines which took away vital winter work opportunities from labourers, were to raise poor law costs and to make men desperate[163]. The response of some vestries was to cut the poor rate, though the rioters had their supporters. One wag noted that at least families ate better Christmas dinners that year as a result of concessions by farmers[164]. Yet in the following four years fires burned in both Creakes as also in Sculthorpe, Stanhoe, Syderstone, Docking, Burnham Overy and beyond; incendiarism was, by a long way, the most popular form of protest. Other acts of protest included the breaking of threshing machines and animal maiming which, in 'troublesome parishes' such as the Creakes[165], continued over some time – to the considerable alarm of local landowners such as Coke. Doubtless shaken by events, he convened meetings of landowners in order to coordinate a response[166].

Some of the protests were against the tithe. Tithe owners were not all clergy; many lay people had acquired the right and clergy were often amenable to demands for the abatement of the rate. Tithe owners benefitted from enclosure awards, often receiving generously more than they were accustomed to receive[167], which intensified opposition to them. Dissenters did not like paying towards a church to which they did not belong, but the precipitating factor was often an unlikely alliance between farmers and labourers; the latter would ask for higher wages which would be promised if tithes could be reduced; labourers were then encouraged to 'mob' or sometimes attack the clergy to obtain concessions to the tithe[168]. (Relations hereabouts were evidently good enough so that this form of protest was absent.) The commutation of tithe from being payment in kind to becoming a fixed money payment in 1836 pacified landowners but marginalised the

---

Flash and a Scare – Incendiarism, Animal Maiming and Poaching in East Anglia 1815-1870, John E. Archer (Oxford 1990) p. 70

[163] Hobsbawm and Rudé (1973) p. 55ff.

[164] Letter to the *Norfolk News* Dec. 30th. 1830 signed 'Swing'

[165] Archer (1990) p 97 & 105 and personal communication

[166] *'A fiendish Outrage'? a Study of Animal Maiming in East Anglia 1830-1870,* John Archer (Agricultural History Review 33 1985) p. 147

[167] Lee (2006) p. 15; Russell (1993) p. 103

[168] Hobsbawm and Rudé (1973) p. 126

labouring classes[169]; the joint effect of enclosure and the commutation of the tithe caused the clergy to be no longer farmers but gentlemen[170]. And while there were clergy who expressed private doubts or even public objections to what was happening, they were by disposition and position likely to counsel obedience to the law[171].

The new Whig Government of 1830, intent on reform, responded by finally relieving individual parishes of the duty to maintain the poor and set up Poor Law Unions. Its purposes and motives were, however, mixed and a degree of perceptive anxiety hovered over the new regime: it was feared that it would 'break up their homes and family connexions, rending them incapable ever of rising from the condition of parochial paupers and prisoners'[172]. South Creake had its own workhouse, established under Gilbert's Act in 1783. The new act brought together 36 parishes for which were provided a single workhouse in Docking. Built in 1835, the first in the county, it was to provide 500 places for the parishes in its locality, which included South Creake. All paupers were to be sent there from the parish; so-called 'outdoor relief' – assistance outside a workhouse, working in the parish – was, in theory, abolished. One of the principle objectives, the reduction in the cost of poor relief was amply achieved[173]: the cost of poor relief in Norfolk almost halved[174]. Resistance was immediate if short-lived: a labourers' strike in nearby Great Bircham drew men from other villages – some hundreds of men took part – and there was considerable violence so that the Dragoons had to be called in and the ringleaders arrested[175]. In practice, residence there was lower in summer[176] when landowners required labourers, and higher in winter when they did not, though even then the population of the Workhouse never exceeded a hundred in those early years. In the years after enclosure, as elsewhere, the population fell by almost a third in the village[177], driven by policies of encouraging emigration both within the country and to the colonies. Those who went were predominantly

---

[169] Tithe Commutation Act 1836; Lee p. (2006) p. 29
[170] Russell (1993) p. 103
[171] Robert Lee (2006) p. 102
[172] *White's Gazetteer and Directory* 1836 p. 629
[173] Robert Lee (2006) p. 82
[174] Archer (1990) p. 50
[175] *Perspectives on Poverty,* Barbara Allen (unpub. dissertation (Cambridge 1990)
[176] White's *History, Gazetteer and Directory* 1845
[177] Bryant (1914) p. 157: population 1861 1058, 1901 747; Neeson (1993) Ch.8

the able and the energetic[178]. At the other extreme the residual population of the workhouse consisted of the old, unmarried mothers, babes in arms and orphan scholars living together in conditions which were supposed to be sufficiently grim to discourage admission[179].

Goggs, like a number of Anglican clergy, was identified with the interests of the large landowners, Lord Townshend and Coke. In particular, he was associated with the enclosure of the common, (from which both he, as a tithe holder and the churchwardens on behalf of the church stood to benefit). Squire Belding of Compton Hall who stood to lose from the Enclosure Award of 1859 directed his executors to have him buried on his own plantation rather than suffer the attentions of the parson and to put on his stone, 'Free from the devil and Parson Goggs', but he survived Goggs by several years. His successor, George Ridsdale is named on the Enclosure Award. Not all clergy took Goggs' hard line; some risked not merely their careers but even their liberty in opposing the application of the poor law (Revd. Ambrose Goode of Terrington wrote a pamphlet on the poor law which nearly caused his arrest for seditious libel[180].) More often 'involvement in every local branch of law making, law enforcement and public administration would inevitably give rise to suspicions that the clergyman was working in his own naked self interest'[181].

By contrast Methodism was popular, in particular, the so-called Primitive Methodist Connexion. Methodism had begun life within the Church, the two Wesleys, John and Charles, being ordained Anglican priests; but the resistance of bishops to their unorthodox methods and the enthusiasm of the groups led to the establishment of Methodist chapels, not all on speaking terms with each other. The Primitive Methodist revival began in Staffordshire in 1807. Its founder, Hugh Bourne, with several others had been expelled from the Methodist Conference because of their open-air revivalist preaching, something which they consciously copied from John Wesley (and from Jesus). They built their first chapel in 1811. By 1823 the

---

[178] Armstrong (2000) p. 23

[179] Docking Workhouse 1881 Census; Lee (2006) p. 81.

[180] E.g. *Customs and Conflict – Some causes of anti-clericalism in Norfolk 1815-1870,* Robert Lee (Rural History CUP 2003) p. 208. Charles Brereton of Massingham and Revd. Henry Holloway of Brancaster were more measured critics of the system.

[181] Lee (2006) p. 101

movement spread to Fakenham[182] and thence to the Creakes. Preachers like Robert Key, a former Yarmouth coal heaver who was stationed at the Fakenham circuit at different times, prided themselves on their contribution to the phenomenal growth of the movement. Unlike its Wesleyan form which was mostly urban and increasingly respectable, Primitive Methodism was a religion predominantly rural and dissociated from class and deference. Jesus Christ was talked about as if he were a farm labourer keeping a family on nine shillings a week[183]. The biblical curse upon those who moved their neighbours' landmark drew loud Amens from congregations. They implicitly and sometimes explicitly challenged the theological justification of a state sponsored church[184]. Men learned to read, to organise and began to communicate with the world outside. So-called Camp meetings in the open air took place in the village but eventually a cottage was converted for the services.

By 1835 the Prims, as they were often called, numbered over 8,000 in Norfolk, growth so rapid as to be an indictment on the state church. By the end of the century there would be scarcely a village in north Norfolk which did not have its chapel. Though the Connexion did not itself engage directly in politics, those many of its members did and its chapels were extensively used for meetings of farm labourers' unions[185] (in spite of national opposition). They were widely believed to foster riots and unrest. This was not surprising since membership of union and chapel overlapped considerably; lay preachers even up to the 1890s were mostly labourers. The National Agricultural Labourers Union, founded in 1872 by a Primitive Methodist preacher, Joseph Arch, was very strong in Norfolk; the South Creake branch, which met in the Chequers Inn, was founded in the same year with 93 men enrolled at the initial meeting[186]. Arch visited the village in July 1877, when he argued the case for solidarity with industrial unions and support for universal suffrage. In the same year, conducting divine service in a Norfolk chapel he spoke of the need to recruit members for the union[187]. Religion and politics were apparently one. Robert Key even claimed to have saved Norfolk from incendiarism. Yet ironically, the very virtues which religion instilled in its adherents: self-discipline, sobriety,

---

[182]*History of the Primitive Methodist Church,* H.B. Kendall (1919) p. 47
[183] *Poor Labouring Men,* Alun Howkins (Routledge 1985) p. 49
[184] Lee (2003) p. 58
[185] Howkins (1985) p. 47
[186] *Eastern Weekly Press* (Norwich) July 6th. 1872
[187] *Eastern Weekly Press* August 11th. 1877

neatness, even eloquence, took them away from the new poor; not everyone took Arch's line. As Wesley himself had said despairingly, 'Everywhere Methodists grow rich'[188]. Trade unionism became, if not more secular, then less closely connected with the chapels. Some meetings took place on the green, including the occasion in May 1913 when the branch was presented by the principal of Bebel House working women's college, Mary Bridges Adams, with a banner emblazoned with the words 'We sow the seed that feeds the world' to which most of the village turned out and the school had the day off[189].

Some idea of the religious affiliation of the village in the nineteenth century can be derived from the 1851 Census data. On census day there were 305 attendances at St. Mary's including 90 children; the Congregational chapel numbered 192 including 64 children; the Methodists, who were still at that time meeting in a converted cottage, numbered 148. (They built their chapel in Back Street in 1883.) The population was 1041[190]. There were thus more non-conformists than members of the established church in village[191], a very rapid development. (In 1932 the chapel joined with the Wesleyan and the United Methodists to form the Methodist Church of Great Britain. It closed in 1979; the Congregational chapel closed in 1973.) The practice of the Roman Catholic faith had been tolerated only since 1829; it appears to have made a brief appearance in the village for in 1878 the Revd. Isaac Bowman refers to the destruction by fire of 'the hurdle barn, so called, but evidently the old Roman Catholic chapel...' No other reference survives.

Another focus of activity, less threatening but nevertheless free from clerical control was the friendly society. The abolition of the gilds had left a gap in village life; they had been, among other things, self-help societies. By the middle of the seventeenth century, some of their functions came to be assumed by so-called friendly societies, which, by the end of the eighteenth century had become so important that legislation was passed regulating them[192]. Meeting in pubs, they sometimes acquired their own premises. Thus was formed in 1844 the South Creake branch of the Oddfellows, styled

---

[188] Howkins (1985) p. 53

[189] *Eastern Weekly Press* May 11th 1913; *School Log Book 1913* p.1.43

[190] Bryant (1914) p. 157

[191] *1851 Census of Religious Worship for Norfolk* (Norfolk Record Society vol. LXII 1998) p. 280-1. The numbers do not take account of those who attended more than once on that day, March 30th. 1851.

[192] *A Social and Economic History of Britain,* Pauline Gregg (Harrrap 1956) p. 315

the 'Rock of Hope'. Oddfellows were based nationally in Manchester. They were influenced by Deist principles 'believing in a supreme being, the creator and preserver of the universe' but clergy often had a leading role as in South Creake. After the annual meeting in July 1868 at the Swan Inn they processed to the Church where the vicar, George Ridsdale, preached on the text 'The rich and the poor meet together; the lord is the maker of them all'[193]. They eventually built a hall at the north end of the village in 1889. Friendly societies were early working men's clubs a subscription to which might support members when ill or injured at work and even ensured a proper burial. They provided a source of welfare that was decided upon by representatives of the contributors, unlike the parish charities which depended upon the whim of the trustees and could be withheld if, for instance, possible recipients were disapproved of because they were members of a trade union. There were hundreds of local friendly societies; over time the Oddfellows tended to absorb them. At its height in the 1870s the national body had an income of £560,000 and the benefits for which it was liable totalled £11,000,000[194]. The advent of state welfare provision deprived it of one of its major functions, though the organisation still continues nationally. The local branch closed in the 1970s having sold its hall some years before.

The parson unlike his Free Church brethren owed his position not to any democratic or congregational principle but to the will of the patron whose right to appoint it was. After the Reformation the advowson, as this right was called, had belonged to the Pepys family in whose family it remained until the eighteenth century when it passed to the Townshends. The level of interest of patrons varied: often members of the family were appointed, a form of nepotism which nevertheless produced surprises[195].

Thus, another area of controversy was education. There had always been those who opposed the education of the poor for fear that they would no longer be biddable workers. Charity schools were opposed in the eighteenth century as a misuse of funds which should be retained within families[196]. It was suggested by the vicar of Stanhoe that education was useless to those in

---

[193] *Eastern Express* (Norwich) July 4th. 1868
[194] Gregg (1956) p. 319; *Fourth Report of the Committee appointed to inquire into Friendly & Benefit Building Societies* 1874 XXIII part 1 xvi-xvii
[195] George Ridsdale and Spencer Compton were both relatives of the Townshends.
[196] One of the reasons for the passing of the Mortmain Act 1736; schools were also thought to undermine dissent: see Jacob (2002) p. 171f.

the station of life 'it has pleased Providence to place the agricultural poor'[197]. Providence was a useful theological standby. Local farmers too recorded their hostility to schools and landowners were known to veto their building. Various attempts had been made to set up a school in the village without success. In 1668, Isaac Lane had left money for a school, but there is no record of its having existed. In 1814, Thomas Scrimshire, still then a curate, recorded his attempts when he first arrived in 1805 to do the same but 'without the least encouragement from [his] richer neighbours so great was their aversion to the education of the poor'; even the churchwardens ignored his appeal for funds towards coals and candles in winter; his wife and daughter managed to keep a Sunday school going but, still lacking the means to obtain books, he appealed to the diocese for assistance in order to 'render essential service to our little scholars'. The villagers, for their part, responded to his initiative by sending some 60 or 70 children whom he had to disappoint[198]. Fortunately, not all potential benefactors took the same view: the year after Scrimshire's letter Thomas Herod left money for a school in North Creake to which South Creake children might go[199].

A school appears to have been established at some point thereafter[200] but it was Ridsdale, who had married into the Townshend family and who was appointed in 1858 who was its champion. Opposing the farming community, he had it rebuilt and took a keen interest in it. He was a non-resident – he was also vicar of Helhoughton near Raynham – but his interest in the village is manifest. (He had the vicarage extended for the benefit of his curate.) The new school was built in 1860 using the old Town house and extending it. It was to be a church school, a so-called

---

[197] Lee (2006) p. 134

[198] Letter dated 1814 in reply to a circular from the diocese of Norwich seeking information about schools. NRO DN/NDS 275/1

[199] *White's History, Gazetteer and Directory* 1845 p. 666

[200] *White's History, Gazetteer and Directory* 1854 p. 662

National School[201]; the funds for its building and running came from the Dorothy Woodhouse and Isaac Lane's charity. The school was said to provide places for 185 children; records show attendance to have ranged about the 100 mark[202]. Ridsdale was a regular and energetic visitor and undertook regular inspections as to the conduct of the school, even visiting the homes of absentees as truant officer. This he did despite the view of a local magistrate and landowner, Sir Willoughby Jones of Cranmer Hall, that education should not be compulsory and that three or four hours a day at school were sufficient[203]. Unlike many local farmers and clergy he took the line that '[i]t was never intended that we should continue in the place and sphere in which we were born' which advancement, he thought, might be assisted by 'getting a little education'[204]. Providence had provided a school. Ridsdale's wife was also a regular visitor (as were many of her successors over the next sixty years, an example of the importance, which became an expectation, of clergy wives). Evening classes were provided for those who were at work, which was attended by some 30 older boys in the early days, and in which Mr. Northam, the head teacher had the assistance of the local shoe mender. The school records give us an unrivalled glimpse of some aspects of the life of the village in those years: the rate of child mortality from diseases such as scarlet fever, typhoid and diphtheria; the conflict in families between the demands of the fields and the need for education; the difficulties of achieving consistent levels of attendance, even though the head was prepared, where necessary, to forego the penny a week subscription[205]. The school flourished throughout the century and much of the next, occasionally outgrowing its premises so that, when evacuees arrived from London during the Second World War, the incomers had to use the Oddfellows Hall.

Ridsdale also had his enemies. He was alleged to have contrived his election as Poor Law Guardian and controlled the election of the Overseer by the vestry. Some felt that he should be preparing for the Sabbath and visiting the

---

[201] *White's History, Gazetteer and Directory* 1864

[202] *South Creake School Log books* 1867-1991

[203] Evidence to *Commission on Employment of Children, Young Persons and Women in Agriculture* (1867-8) British Parliamentary Papers (Irish University Press) vol. 10 Appendix Pt. II p. 58; see also *Eastern Weekly Press* Oct. 5th. 1867

[204] An anonymous letter in *Eastern Weekly Press* October 5th. 1867

[205] *School Log books* December 1867 and Jan 10th 1870

sick rather than exercising a political role[206]. Such was the suspicion with which even conscientious clergy were regarded.

Church Schools were to be the last institution in parishes over which the Church still had influence. Their responsibilities for the poor law and for highways were handed over to the new local authorities, highways in 1862 and the poor law in 1894[207]. Clergy were chairmen of the managers of the school and heavily involved in its governance; their engagement with the children varied enormously. It has been suggested that the involvement of the church in education was an instrument of control rather than intended to benefit the children of the village[208], but in South Creake at least the Non-conformist Sunday School treats took precedence over school attendance and seems not then to have been a point of contention. Thomas Seppings, churchwarden, lent them a field for the purpose.

Amidst the vagaries of human interaction, the Church was no less subject to the forces of nature or 'Acts of God' as the insurance companies used to have it. In the autumn of 1859 the church was struck by lightning, not for the first time. The damage was evidently considerable and it was fortunate that the church benefited from being insured. Another change, more predictable, that towards the Church becoming more of a voluntary society was the abolition of the compulsory church rate in 1868. The change, however, had been anticipated: by 1859 a voluntary subscription had effectively replaced the rate which had, at least in the case of Squire Belding, become impossible to collect[209]. The effect was to increase the income of the church by more than 50%. (By 1905 'subscriptions' had become 'collections' taken in church.)

Ridsdale also saw the arrival of an organ in the church. Bought in 1868 from Bevingtons of London, it was evidently a gift since no record appears in the church accounts. Organs enabled a better standard of music; they also displaced local musicians, often a source of dissension. At Walsingham two years previously, dissenters had gone so far as to blow up the new instrument which had arrived four years earlier[210]. In South Creake they enabled the employment of an organ blower and the playing of the newly

---

[206] A letter to the *Eastern Express* (Norwich) March 28th 1868

[207] Local Government Act 1894 s. 6 transferred non-ecclesiastical powers of vestries to parish councils.

[208] Lee (2006) p.133; both dissenters and trade unionists held this view.

[209] *Churchwardens Account Book* 1789-1929

[210] Lee (2003) p. 201

popular range of hymns. The first standard hymn book was published in 1861; previously most singing was of metrical psalms. But this new professionalism in the taking of services, because it displaced lay involvement, removed an important element of participation in worship[211].

Meanwhile, outside the building other changes in village life were afoot. The Agricultural Revolution of the nineteenth century, of which Coke was a prominent exponent and populariser, did not much include the use of machinery (apart from the controversial threshing machine) or the use of synthetic chemicals; its greater intensity in fact required more labour. For a while this resulted in the recruitment of itinerant gangs of women and children (used largely for weeding, hoeing and stone picking and at harvest) employed by independent gangmasters, such that their poor conditions of work were raised in Parliament and became the subject of regulatory legislation[212]. In some villages it was impossible to find housing because of the control of land exercised by a dominant landlord; this meant that 'open' villages like Docking, where there were many landowners, became overcrowded with labourers seeking work. Labour was seasonal and, by comparison with the towns, badly paid.

Some attempt was made on the part of landowners to address the problems of poverty. The Docking Union Agricultural Association, formed in 1839 had as its object 'the providing and rewarding of good conduct and encouragement of habits of industry and frugality of servants, labourers and cottagers' and arranged annual competitions for ploughing and hedging, shepherding, and even sewing and knitting in the village. The problem of the farm labourer as identified by its chairman, Sir Willoughby Jones, was debt which, he averred, was caused partly by household improvidence and partly by the activities of aggressive hawkers selling worthless goods; he advocated the establishment of cooperative stores in the villages, but nothing came of it[213]. A more adversarial approach was the attempt to secure decent and stable wages.

Trade Unions had become legal in 1824, but the courts presided over by farmer magistrates found ways of prosecuting members[214] and only in 1872,

---

[211] Russell (1993) p. 111

[212] *Report on Employment of Women an Children in Agriculture* (BPP vol. 6 1843); *Sixth Report of the Children's Employment Commission* (BPP 1867); Gangs Act 1867

[213] *Eastern Weekly Express* October 12th 1867

[214] The 'Tolpuddle Martyrs' were transported in 1834 for taking 'unlawful oaths'.

following further permissive legislation[215], was an agricultural union formed. Joseph Arch's trade union came to South Creake that same year; the first union meeting reported the sacking of men who disputed their wages. In the years that followed strikes grew in number, sometimes opposed nationally. 'As always, it was the weather and the state of agriculture in each tiny local world that really determined action.'[216] Nor could the union resist the onset of the great agricultural depression which began in 1874 which left farms unlet, rents reduced (by nearly a half on Lord Leicester's lands)[217] and some of the big houses empty. As wheat prices fell with cheap foreign imports, land was laid down to grass. With the slight improvement in agriculture of the 1880s the national union faded, and when conditions worsened again farmers organised themselves and coordinated wage reductions. The strikes of 1891-2 were very bitter, such that preachers from the same chapel, farmer and labourer, could be permanently estranged[218]. At Burnham Thorpe strikers stopped others at work and hung their harrow from a tree, but to no avail. They went back to work for 1s. a week less. Until the establishment of a national wages board[219], strikes, lock-outs and the blacklisting of strikers scarred village life. The war years brought no respite until wages were eventually fixed in 1917 but their deregulation again in 1921 led to the last great strike of 1923, when Bishop Pollock attempted to bring the parties together at his Palace in Norwich[220] but without success.

Attempts to unite villages in a common interest were made by both landowners and clergy. Christmas charitable dinners and the provision of clothing in winter were commonly noted in local newspapers, and the church harvest 'festival' became common. The latter was revived in 1843 by a Cornish parson named Hawker and, such was its popularity that in 1862 Convocation issued a form of service. It replaced the more secular Harvest Home and those clergy who introduced it were sometimes known contemptuously as 'horkeys'. On the whole harvest festivals were very popular, though according to a member of the Norwich diocesan conference

---

[215] The Trade Union Act 1871
[216] Howkins (1985) p. 80
[217] Ibid. p. 2
[218] Ibid. p. 173
[219] By the Agricultural Wages Act 1924
[220] Howkins (1985) p. 159

in 1902, 'the clergy had lost the influence they once had over the agricultural labourer'[221].

War, ritualism and depopulation (1905-1992)

With the secularisation of local government following the Local  Government Act of 1894 the role of the church gradually altered; the vestries, from being the administrative body of the parish, had become purely ecclesiastical bodies. Spencer Compton's long and uneventful tenure as vicar witnessed that transition. Just before it, the vestry voted for application for a new main road to be made between Fakenham and Burnham 'between the two railway stations'[222] both now gone. Compton was an ardent evangelical (and was sympathetic towards the Congregational minister), a reader of international events such as the fate of Armenia, and of the Jews and Protestants in Russia[223]. What his parishioners made of this is unsure.

In 1905 John Scully arrived; he was a former Roman Catholic and married while he was in post; his wife played the organ and ran the Sunday school. It was he who converted the heating from coke to oil.

Scully's incumbency encompassed a yet larger and, to the village, utterly unexpected event, the so-called Great War from 1914-1918, which was to bring down many of the great houses of England and kill millions of its young men. Scully rallied enthusiastically to the cause in print and published whatever details he had of the young men whom he had encouraged to volunteer. He organised fundraising for the Prince of Wales

---

[221] Howkins (1985) p. 83; *Eastern Weekly Press* 12th April 1902

[222] Vestry book August 1st. 1889

[223] *Parish Magazine* 1885-1905 (NRO/PD612/14-41

62

Relief Fund and for hospital garments for the wounded to be made in the parish. His thrice weekly services of intercession continued throughout the hostilities. To the first battle of the Somme in July 1916, Scully responded with thanksgiving that the 'great offensive' had been 'so successful', in fact, it took seven men, five from the same regiment, from the village (and almost half a million infantrymen from the British Army). Two of the funerals took place in the village, occasions of overwhelming solidarity in sorrow[224]. One of them was that of Fred Hunter, who had assisted only months before in helping to extinguish a fire in the Church while on leave. A detachment of the Warwickshire Regiment was billeted at the brewery site during the war. With the loss of young men into the services here as elsewhere soldiers on leave as well as young boys released from school early were used on the land. Meanwhile the headmaster of the school, Chute Thompson, had volunteered and survived to return to the village in 1919; he suffered with malaria thereafter[225]. Scully appears to have suffered from declining health and he left the parish in 1920, after which it was cared for first by curates from nearby churches.

After this interregnum, there came to South Creake the Revd. Charles Hepworth. No external event troubled his ministry but rather it was marked by a changed understanding of what it was to be the church in England. It had been long in coming. The Revd. John Keble, at the opening of the Oxford Assizes in 1833, had preached about what he called national apostasy, epitomised by the decline in religious observance and the need for a revival. His Assize Sermon caught a mood. The revival of which he spoke drew on contemporary scholarly work on the life and teaching of the early church as also on its mediaeval

---

[224] Fred Hunter and Frederick George are buried in the churchyard; eight have no known grave. Fred Hunter's funeral is described in the *Parish Magazine* (August 1917): NRO PD 612/41

[225] *South Creake School Log Books* (as above)

successor. The Church was not, on this view, to be regarded as an arm of the State[226] as the Reformation seemed to have made it, but as a divine society continuous with not only the earliest church but also with the Roman Catholic Church, which had only recently been officially recognised in England. The Oxford Movement, as it became known, affected church building, the interiors of churches and the forms of worship, the training of clergy and their style of life. In this its members sought to imitate, both in ritual and in theology, what was believed Church life to have been like before the Reformation. Like the Prims, if from an entirely different point of view, its adherents sought freedom from state control. The difference between their ideal and the reality was that the medieval church was a powerful counterbalance to the state. The nineteenth century church was rapidly losing its secular authority, effectively leaving its leaders a choice between social protest and withdrawal into those areas over which it still had control. Ritualism had several faces: its practitioners introduced candles, coloured vestments and incense, high mass and auricular confession, and in urban slum parishes many combined this with engagement with the physical conditions of their parishioners; in the countryside it was true that it was more difficult to engage with the 'secret life of the rural poor'[227], but to be aware was a start. On the other hand the ritualists were regarded with suspicion by rural non-conformity, and it was easier for those who held such views to pay attention to the building, to liturgical and ecclesial correctness and to the exclusion of those who did not agree. The movement has been described, on the one hand, as a retreat into fantasy and myth[228] or, on the other to express an austere devotion and a theological engagement with the world. It could be either. It certainly made worship more visual, by intention the worship of heaven as of earth.

Hepworth's appointment was secured by the Dowager Marchioness Townshend, her son the Marquis being a minor; she was a Roman Catholic which may account for the appointment. He very quickly introduced the

---

[226] Ironically, Keble's sermon was a protest against the suppression of Anglican bishoprics in Catholic Ireland.

[227] *To the Edge of Triumph – A Study of Charles Marson,* Reg. Groves (Jubilee 1985) p. 14 Marson was a gifted Anglo Catholic priest in the early years of the twentieth century who worked in inner London, Romney Marshes and in rural Devon.

[228] *A Case of Cultural Distortion,* Valerie Pitt in *Essays Catholic and Radical* ed. Leech and Williams (Bowerdean 1983) p. 205ff: '... [they] made religion a life substitute rather than a life revealer...'

pattern of early communion and Sung Eucharist - at the latter only the celebrant communicated; incense and the wearing of cassocks by the choir were introduced within six months (incense was first used on Christmas day 1921); before long there was a daily mass followed by matins and, twice a week, the litany; on his first Good Friday he instituted the Three Hours devotion. He reinstated the side altars; the Angelus was rung and the Stations of the Cross were instituted in the church; he took down the Georgian Coat of Arms and the Ten Commandments intending to replace them with a Rood. His cavalier attitude towards his work is summed up in a letter he wrote to the Chancellor of the diocese: "Please kindly supply us with a general covering faculty to cover all changes in the future....I suppose this will cost more, but is cheapest in the long run with a church like South Creake."[229] His application for a Rood was refused. He was, it seems, an indefatigable visitor and, in spite of his Catholic views, broad in his sympathies and rather fun. A parishioner said of him "Yes, we know he antics, but we loike him, so we antics with him"[230]. It was presumably at his instigation that the parish raised money for the strike fund in 1923 in support of agricultural labourers[231]. When he visited chapel goers, he would say 'I don't mind where you go as long as you go somewhere[232]. If collections are anything to go by he was a huge hit with the village. Numbers of communicants at festivals doubled[233].

His sudden departure for Australia in July 1924 left the parish in the hands of a succession of curates. Fr. Clarence Porter, drafted in as curate in charge from Blakeney continued the tradition if anything more punctiliously, apparently without upsetting people[234], but he only stayed a year before Hepworth returned only to leave finally for South Africa the following year. (When Hepworth died in 1936 his body was brought back to be buried in South Creake churchyard.) He was followed as locum by Fr. Arthur Leeds who became curate of the neighbouring parish of Little Walsingham, though living in the vicarage. His vicar, Alfred Hope Patten, was to found the

[229] *Eastern Daily Press* Sept. 11th. 1922

[230] *In Praise of Norfolk*, ed. Mervyn Horder (Alistair Press 1988)

[231] *South Creake Register of Services* April 5th. 1923

[232] *Memories of St. Mary's Church, South Creake*, Marie Barnes (1989)

[233] *Churchwardens Account Book* 1789-1929; *Register of Services* April 1st.1923: there were 90 Easter communicants compared with 43 in 1919; on an ordinary Sunday at the Sung Mass there were 70-80 non-communicating worshippers.

[234] Congregations if anything rose: on Easter Day 1925, there were 95 communicants, 120 worshippers at morning services: *Register of Services* 1925

Anglican shrine of our Lady of Walsingham in 1931, and came to preach at St. Mary's from time to time. Between them Porter and Leeds did 'the real work to "catholicize" the parish', apparently[235].

Hepworth's successor, Henry Bernard Ventham (1927-1944), developed the Walsingham connection and High Church practice further. Ventham was a man of some means, who was able to put his ideas into visible form. His background was unusual. He was among those clergy who were concerned about the validity of Anglican orders which had been pronounced null and void by Pope Leo XIII in an encyclical of 1896. Thus in 1898 Ventham had got himself ordained (and, in 1903 and again in 1905, consecrated bishop of Dorchester) by one Joseph René Villatte, a Catholic excommunicate who, under the name of Mar Timotheus, had founded the Order of Corporate Reunion, an organisation intended to achieve reunion of the churches by ensuring the validity of clergy ordination[236]. (Because Villatte himself had been ordained by a bishop of the Malankara Syrian Orthodox church, this apparently ensured that Ventham was himself validly ordained!) Ventham is hence the only incumbent of the parish to have been in canonical if irregular Episcopal orders. In 1922 however he was ordained as an Anglican by the bishop of London.

Ventham was the last vicar to be appointed by the Townshends; apparently short of money the Dowager Marchioness was proposing to sell the advowson to a Protestant trust and it was only due to the exertions of a former resident of the village, Clifford Sheringham, that the English Church Union bought the patronage which it vested it in the Guild of All Souls in 1944[237]. He upgraded some of the makeshift changes to the interior of the building made by Hepworth, erecting a stone altar and wrenching out the Victorian pews[238] so that the rubble floor had to be remade with tiles, or pamments, taken from estate houses at Holkham; like Hepworth he failed in his attempt to get a rood installed. He introduced the Reserved Sacrament, (which he removed whenever the bishop visited, to the disgust of some of the parishioners[239]). He was the final straw for James Griggs whose father had been churchwarden since Compton's day, and who had himself been ten

---

[235] *Parish Record Book* written up by the Reverend L.H.M. Smith 1956/7

[236] *Bishops at Large,* Peter Anson (Faber 1963) p.83; *The Order of Corporate Reunion,* Bertil Persson (Sweden 2000)

[237] *Parish Record Book* (as above)

[238] These were installed in 1853: *Register of Services* 1853

[239] Marie Barnes (ibid.)

years in office throughout Hepworth's reign but fell out very badly with Ventham. Contemporary records give the impression of a somewhat embattled church set against 'the destructive opposition engineered by non-conformists and non-churchgoers'[240]; 'The parish... in his eyes was a sort of ecclesiastical peculiar, of an East Anglian petit église of which he was the primate[241]'. With regard to the school 'seeing that more than 60% of the children at the schools were non-conformists' he could not 'justify their existence as Church schools'[242]; he seems to have ceased either to visit or serve on the managers of the school. It was during his incumbency that the church became a recipient of charity rather than a dispenser of it. The congregation plummeted during his regime[243].

Ventham, a man of strong and unswerving opinions, died in office in 1944; his remains were placed under the John the Baptist altar just as the B-17 Flying Fortresses which had daily droned over the village from RAF Sculthorpe also departed but in their case only for another airbase. Norfolk's war was fought largely in the air and there were six RAF airfields within fifteen miles of the village, several of them served by US squadrons. De Havilland Mosquitoes could also be seen in the skies, as GIs were observed beating up the lanes, and the occasional marauding enemy fighter terrified villagers in the street, one local replying defiantly if impotently with a shotgun. Fear of invasion, once acute, gradually faded.

Father Michael Smith, Ventham's successor, was vicar of the parish for thirty three years. By the time of his arrival rural England, following D-Day, was acquiring, in addition to its mass of airfields a host of POW camps as numbers of surrendering Axis military arrived from France. There were some five hundred of them, including several nearby. Fr. Smith took a pastoral interest in German POWs and maintained a pastoral contact with one of them for some years afterwards, attempting to secure his return after the war from Soviet occupied territory. (The correspondence reveals the highly sectarian nature of his religion as well as his loneliness.)[244]. He married a number of village GI brides just after the war.

---

[240] *Church Vestry Book* 1935

[241] Anson (1963) p. 273

[242] *School Managers' Minute Book* Oct. 29th 1928; he ceased to attend meetings or to visit the school shortly thereafter.

[243] In 1924 there were 99 Christmas communicants; in 1938 there were 22.

[244] *Friendly Foe; the letters of Leo Schnitter a German POW in England,* Martin Parsons (Peterborough 2000).

He also devoted much time to the improvement of the church; his attention to detail was considerable. The 14th and 15th century glass was rearranged and all but five of the windows releaded. One of them was dedicated to his mother and included the petition that those seeing it should 'Pray for [her] soul...'. Her son thereby managed to achieve legal status[245] for prayers for the dead, something which the Reformers had removed from the liturgy, so long, it was decided, as it did not suggest belief in purgatory but merely desired the repose of the deceased's soul, 'until the resurrection'. The nave roof was repaired and the angels restored, repainted and some given new wings. He had all the woodwork treated against death watch beetle. He it was who established the tradition of flowers in the church, much appreciated by visitors. Unlike his predecessor, he was a regular visitor to the school, as well as chairman of the managers; he required that each day in term time two children would go to church at noon to ring the Angelus. Mr. Billington, headteacher from 1955 to 1964 was churchwarden for most of that time. Fr. Smith established the Visitors' Day, the patronal festival, when guest preachers, some of renown, would attract large numbers to pray and to engage socially, fed and watered by women of the congregation. The church was very much on the ecclesiastical map.. Pilgrims came in busloads through much of the year, while the local congregation, largely non-communicating, was small[246]; he appears to have been latterly an unfulfilled and isolated man. His sudden death in 1977 marked symbolically the next major change in the life of the village.

Fr. Nicholas Bundock, who was appointed as priest-in-charge prior to re-organisation of the parishes, was very active in the village and his involvement in the school was much valued. He was the first married priest with children for nearly sixty years. He claimed to have given the church back to the village. It was he who obtained the rood from a redundant church in Colchester and had it installed in the chancel arch and without having to go to

---

[245] *Re South Creake P.C.C.* [1959] 1 All E.R. p. 197 (Butterworths)

[246] *Register of Services* 1944-78. In early days attendance at the two morning services would be in the region of 50; latterly this fell to fewer than 30.

law. But he did not stay. Nor did his successor the hirsute Lloyd Gedge who went back to Canada where his wife came from. One reorganisation was

 followed by another: originally grouped with North Creake and then Waterden and then again with the Barshams to cope with falling clergy numbers, the diocese decided only a few years later to substitute Syderstone and Sculthorpe for the Barshams. Both the combination of differing churchmanships and the feeling of constant change were unsettling factors. Meanwhile numbers in school and children in the village were beginning to drop. The school finally closed in 1991, but the writing had been on the wall for some time.

Agricultural practices had developed apace. The development of artificial weed killers, the arrival first of the reaper-binder and then of the diesel tractor and the combine harvester began seriously to erode the size of the labour force. On Bluestone Farm in 1930 the Alley brothers were among the first in the country to introduce them. Others were slow to follow and horses were still in use until after the Second World War. But by the end of the 1950s the largest labour force in the village had become redundant; children's harvest holidays were a thing of the past. The advent of the grain dryer meant that the time of harvest was no longer at the behest of the heavens. Industry, whether agriculturally related or manufacturing, like the razor blade factory in the old brewery[247] and which was very successful in its heyday, came and went.

Stability, one of the hallmarks of village life had gone. So had many of the facilities upon which the communities had traditionally relied. In 1883, the village boasted a church school with 165 pupils on roll, two blacksmiths, a carpenter, three butchers, a saddler, five pubs, a brewery, a post office, two grocer's, a baker's, a tailor's and a draper's shop, all to support the village[248]. Now, the labourers have gone elsewhere; their cottages have been bought by

---

[247] The Ace Razor blade Factory lasted from 1925 to 1951.
[248] *Kelly's Gazetteer and Directory* 1883

second home owners[249]; the shops have all closed; the school is gone; the Prims, the Congs and the Oddfellows too; one pub remains – and a church. Even clergy had become less of a fixture: three came and went in fifteen years. Many streets are empty outside holiday periods. Those who live in the village have cars and can find other places in which to occupy their leisure hours. Villages are no longer administrative units; their parish councils are amenity bodies with consultative powers. In many places, they are not much more than dormitories. Clergy have long ceased to be officials within local government structures which are organised much more centrally than hitherto. With each loss of involvement so the role of country clergy has changed; if they entered local politics it was simply as members of the public with no succession; increasingly they have become providers of ritual events, expositors of scripture and amateur counsellors. The occasional offices allow the biggest opportunity for engagement. To penetrate further into private lives is difficult.

Retrospect and prospect

History thus turns imperceptibly into memory. We ask, in the light of all of this, where we are now. Events come now too close to make judgments, but close enough to take decisions.

For more than a thousand years, the church has presided over the civil and religious turmoils of English society. Its contribution towards the sustenance of faith and hope in the community seems evident from the affection shown to the building, but the character and practical expression of that faith has changed as if from world to world. It was an agent of reconciliation between the colonial Norman overlords and the English people; it contributed, in a minor way, to a military defence of that faith; it offered solace and hope through its practical interpretation of mortality; it was a forum of debate over the endemic issues of the distribution of property and power. It marshalled and channelled the growing abilities of a mobile laity in the years up to the coming of the Tudors; it even coped with the Reformations of the sixteenth and seventeenth centuries; it increasingly regulated the conduct of parishioners between each other. As always some people were formed by their religion, some made of it an instrument of their own purposes.

---

[249] 30% of homes according to the 2001 Census

Arguably the most disruptive factor, long in coming, was caused by division: the arguments were no longer conducted, as it were, within the family; sometimes more successfully often less so community life was conducted on a tribal and eventually on a more secular, individualistic basis. Parish life

became intrinsically unstable. Partly for this reason, some men tired of religion as the source of wisdom as also new knowledge slowly marginalised it. The combination of egalitarianism and rational thought proved potent. The Church's response to rapid social change was moreover ambiguous: clergy were too often 'instruments of secular authority in nineteenth-century rural life'; and, in spite of the efforts of some, they were often heartily despised by their parishioners[250], occupying as they did a particular niche in the social stratum which set them apart from the least of their brethren. Some encouraged education, some contributed to the knowledge revolution in print (though their learning did not always equip them to minister in parishes). A few took up the cause of the poor, some quietly, some at risk of their position even their liberty; most fulfilled their role as conduits of national and regional policy, often acting as magistrates, commissioners of one sort or another as well as administering the poor law. Victorian religion was still a matter of social duty, but the divisions between churches represented fissures in society and when these fissures could not be bestridden they found secular expression.

The churches emerged apparently unscathed from the shock of the Great War[251] which seriously dislocated rural life. Spencer Compton was the last of the gentlemen clergy. In their place there arose the professional clergyman whose standards of conduct, however, were never properly regulated. No longer a part of the administration of the civil parish, no longer a gentleman, no longer a dispenser of goodwill to the poor, some, sought a maverick

---

[250] Lee (2003) p. 197

[251] 'Churchgoing had ceased to be an accepted duty or even a social obligation [but...] it had been followed by the erection of no commonly accepted spiritual value.': Pauline Gregg (1956) p. 545

expression of the faith which was marred not by its faux medievalism but by its occasional bouts of bigotry.

Now, with the decline of the Catholic movement, its fragmentation over the ordination of women, which was approved by General Synod in 1992, the foreseeable consecration of women bishops, and the amalgamation of parishes of different character in the benefice, the future of its tradition might be thought to be in question. The Visitors' Day has long ceased. The church building, with its slightly tawdry statues and faded splendour, houses a smallish but faithful congregation, augmented by the occasional holiday maker and second home owner. During the week it speaks to the many casual visitors who enter through its unlocked doors; some of them on pilgrimage to Walsingham, some to look, some to pray. In the summer the church welcomes an increasing number of concert goers who come to hear something of Europe's rich Christian heritage of music. How far it registers with them that the building is a house of prayer and the holy words sung at concerts have meaning is hard to say. The building still makes an emphatic visual statement of what it is about, but whether what it says can now be read is unclear. More widely, the utter collapse of rural non-conformity, once so vigorous, raises questions about the Christian project in England.

Our Christian culture is now much less evident: in our institutions, in our language or in our social observances. The purveyors of information are many of them ignorant of that culture. Those brought up in it are no longer prepared to transmit it. There are now many competing voices and many claims to attention the result of which is the relativisation of all cultural symbols. The faith, when presented, is normally set in the context of the challenges to it: Darwin's theory of evolution, propounded over a hundred and fifty years ago, has replaced secular socialism as the major explication of human interaction. That Darwinism does not answer questions about human purposes and lacks any coherent ethical equipment has not entirely escaped notice. In any case, controversy is assumed to be more interesting than the laborious explication of principles. As to human purposes, they are widely held to be incapable of any common answer. People must decide for themselves without help. Liberalism accords equal status to those who have their hands on the levers of power, marginalising all other ideologies. Meanwhile government encourages a sort of ecumenism by dealing with what it calls 'faith communities', recognising their occasional usefulness while no longer paying heed to their differing claims.

As to the Church's capacity to make people good, that remains unproven: good intentions and forms of good practice have been chronically corrupted and theology has often been put that the service of expediency; it was ever thus but the climate is now peculiarly hostile. Christians remain disproportionately involved in good works. Meanwhile, the vital doctrines of sin and forgiveness are often rejected by society in practice if not in principle; our pundits are selective as to who is characterised as a sinner and who may be forgiven. A blame culture allows only certain people to start again. A therapeutic culture is disinclined to listen to moral challenge and the church, less confident rarely speaks either the grammar or the vocabulary of morality. The great Protestant alternative, the major plank of the Reformation, that we are not saved by being good but by believing – radical though it is – does not satisfy the great number who think that religion is about other people behaving well, even if we ourselves are bad at it. It is all very confusing.

It does seem rather an important time not to lose our nerve. We may have to hang on and wait for better times, but arguably there is more than that to be done. Ecologically speaking there are what are called centres of endemism, places of hugely rich biodiversity which act as reservoirs of animal and plant species when the climate is unfavourable against the day when things improve and they can multiply and spread into newly available lands. The church likewise grows in parched ground but in its possession of a heritage of visual worship, a discipline of prayer and a rule of life, it is an untapped reservoir of equivalent richness. Its penitential discipline, its daily prayer, its teaching on the life of meditation, its practice of adoration focussed on visible signs of the invisible God, its understanding of the Eucharistic sacrifice, its huge body of teaching on social and spiritual matters alike: it would be tragic to discard them.

It is true that some aspects of our heritage have become attenuated. That applies in particular to the matters of spirituality in which there is now quite wide interest. Many modern resources of spirituality tend to be individualistic and easily discarded. The Church's spirituality, by contrast, is based on its belief that human beings are called. That idea, though hugely counter-cultural, is fundamental implying as it does a sense of accountability to God, rather than his being merely a source of reassurance. Prayer was traditionally understood as a kind of work, the work of God, rather than a means of relaxation or refreshment, a fearful encounter with Him who is all justice and all mercy. The inner life, an unexplored realm for many and denied by some, is that which makes us fully human because it frees us in a way that nothing else can.

Along with the need to renew these practices as the bases for the moral life, there is a clear need for re-evaluation and development, not least in sexual matters. The Church at large has been taken by surprise by the sexual revolution and its inner weakness has been mirrored by failures of compassion and understanding. Likewise, our stewardship of the earth and its plenty raises huge questions about our destruction of a resource over which we have increasingly control not matched by greater reverence for its Giver. Less controversial doctrinally but not practically, is the need to address the fundamental and widespread problem of greed.

Thus, the theology of virtue, based upon faith, provides a practical and coherent basis for living more sophisticated than the blunt tool of human rights which latter, because it embraces believer and unbeliever, is widely accepted. In fact it will not do the job, not only because it shows every sign of becoming oppressive but also because, without faith, such rights cannot be shown to exist. Whereas the old virtues, courage and fairness, humility and loyalty, moderation and wisdom, faith, hope and love and their allies, the gifts of the Spirit, are the basis for a more rounded if challenging morality.

As for the sense of community, on which Christian identity is based, it is in principle more capable of practical expression in a village than in a town, but this requires a focus and a forum for mutual encouragement as well as devotion by parish priests made much harder now that they are so thinly spread. Village life requires bridge-builders as much as anywhere else. Communities have to have some regulatory framework, however loose, more compelling than the police as well as a sense of themselves which remembers that they have a context. But if faith, both in its inwardness and its social demands, is to mean anything it must be talked about outside the narrow confines of a church service. Worship has to be that which we offer not only what we attend.

The Church's perennial task is how to regulate the relationship between its title purposes and the character and priorities of the society in which it is set, so that it does more than merely collude with the presuppositions of the age. As we have seen participation in powerful structures exerts huge pressure; lack of influence leads to different temptations, seeking the alleged certainties of the past or being blown along by every wind of fashion. We believe that to God alone is worship due and the quest for holiness is a prerequisite to the survival of the life of faith, perhaps even to the hope of the people. Without it strategies, analyses, programmes, courses, publicity campaigns, appeals, even sermons and prayers are, as Piers Plowman wrote, a piecrust.

Roger Arguile, St. Thomas Aquinas 2011

References

Allen, Barbara, *Perspectives on Poverty* (unpub. dissertation Cambridge 1990)

Anson, Peter, *Bishops at Large* (Faber 1963)

Archer, John, 'A *Fiendish Outrage'? a Study of Animal Maiming in East Anglia 1830-1870* (Agricultural History Review 33 1985)

_____ *By a Flash and a Scare – Incendiarism, Animal Maiming and Poaching in East Anglia 1815-1870* (Oxford 1990)

Armstrong, Alan, '*Population 1700-1950'* in *Norwich since 1550* (Continuum 2004)

_____ *The Population of Victorian and Edwardian Norfolk,* (University of East Anglia 2000)

Bainbridge, Virginia, *Gilds in the Medieval Countryside 1350-1558* (Woodbridge 1996)

Bedingfield A.L., *Cartulary of Creake Abbey* (Norfolk Records Society 1966)

Bennett, H.S., *Life on the English Manor 1150-1400* (Cambridge 1937)

Blomefield, Francis and Charles Parkin, *An Essay toward a topographical history of Norfolk* (1806) (vol. VII)

British Parliamentary Papers: (1843) *Employment of Women and Children in Agriculture* (18430; Sixth *Report of the Children's Employment Commission –Agricultural Gangs* (1867); First *Report from the Employment of Children, Young Persons and Women in Agriculture* (1867-8) (Irish University Press 1969)

Brown (née Barnes), Marie, Memories *of St. Mary's Church South Creake* (1989)

Bryant T. Hugh, *The Churches of Norfolk – Hundred of Brothercross* (Norwich Mercury 1914)

Clanchy M., *From Memory to Written Record 1066-1307* (Blackwell 1993)

Crowley J. and Reid A., *The Poor Law in Norfolk 1700-1850* (Ely 1983)

Dyer, Christopher ed., *The Self-Contained Village?* (Hertfordshire 2007)

Duffy, Eamon, *The Stripping of the Altars* (Yale 1992)

Eastern Weekly Express/Eastern Express/Eastern Weekly Press (Norwich 1867-1918)

Fincham, Kenneth and Tyacke, Nicholas, *Altars Restored: The Changing Face of English Religious Worship 1547-c.1700* (OUP 2007)

Gregg, Pauline, *A Social and Economic History of Britain* (Harrap 1956)

Haig, Christopher, *English Reformations* (OUP 1992)

Hesse, Mary, *Medieval Field Systems and Land Tenure in South Creake* (Norfolk Archaeology vol. 43 1998)

Hobsbawm E.J. & Rudé George, *Captain Swing* (Penguin 1973)

Howard F.E., *The Mediaeval Styles of the English Parish Church* (Batsford 1936)

Howkins Alun, *Poor Labouring Men* (Routledge 1985)

Jacob W.M., *Lay People and Religion in the early Eighteenth Century* (Cambridge 2002)

Jewson C.B., *The Jacobin City (*Blackie 1975)

Jungmann, Joseph, *Mass of the Roman Rite* (Burns & Oates 1959)

Kendall H.B., *History of the Primitive Methodist Church* (1919)

Knowles, Dom David, *The Religious Orders in England* vols. II & III (Cambridge 1959)

Kumin, Beat, *The Shaping of a Community* (Scolar Press 1996)

Leach, A.F., *English Schools at the Reformation* (London 1896)

Lee, Robert, *Customs and Conflict – Some causes of anti-clericalism in Norfolk 1815-1870* (Rural History CUP 2003)

____ *Rural Society and the Anglican Clergy 1815-1914* (Boydell 2006)

Mason R.H., A *History of the County of Norfolk* (1884)

Maltby, Judith, *Prayer Book and People in Elizabethan and Early Stuart England* (Cambridge 1998)

Moreton, C.E., *The Townshends and their World* (Cambridge 1992)

Myers A.R., *English Historical Documents 1327-1485*, (Routledge 1995)

Neeson, J.M., *Commoners: Common Right, Enclosure and Social Change in England, 1700-1820* (Cambridge 1993)

Norfolk News (Norwich) 1823-1917

Orme, Nicholas, *Medieval Schools: from Roman Britain to Tudor England* (Yale 2006)

Page, William, *A History of Norfolk* ed. (Victory County History 1906)

Pantin, W.A., *The English Church in the Fourteenth Century* (Cambridge) 1955)

Parker R.A.C., Coke *of Norfolk - A Financial and Agricultural Study 1707-1842* (Oxford 1975)

Pevsner, Nikolaus and Bill Wilson, *Buildings of England - Norfolk vol. 2* (Penguin 1971)

Pitt, Valerie, in *Essays Catholic & Radical* ed. Leech & Williams (Bowerdean 1983)

Platt, Colin, *The Parish Churches of Medieval England* (Secker and Warburg 1981)

Pooley, Graham, *Eleven Hundred Years – South Creake* (1985)

Pounds, N.J.G., *A History of the English Parish* (Cambridge 2000)

Powell Edgar, *The Rising in East Anglia in 1381* (Cambridge 1896)

Rawcliffe, C. and Wilson, P. eds., *Norwich since 1550* (Continuum 2004)

Runciman, *History of the Crusades,* (Cambridge 1951-4)

Russell, Anthony, *The Country Parson* (SPCK 1993)

Tawney, R.H., *The Agrarian Problem of the Sixteenth Century* (London 1912)

Thomas Hugh M., *The English and the Normans* (Oxford 2003)

Thompson, E.P., *The Making of the English Working Class* (Penguin 1968)

Tyerman C.J., *England and the Crusades* (Chicago 1988)

_____ *God's War* (Penguin 2007)

Young, Arthur, *General View of the Agriculture of Norfolk,* (1804)

Many of the above books were obtained through Wells Public Library or seen at the Millennium and Kings Lynn Public Libraries to whose ever helpful staff grateful thanks are offered. Copies of newspapers were seen at the Norwich offices of the Eastern Daily Press whose assistance is likewise acknowledged. Some parish records, not recorded above, are in the possession of the parish. Other documents are found in the Norfolk Records Office, as indicated. My thanks are due to its efficient and helpful staff.

Rectors /Vicars

Year	Name	Patron
1152	John de Sucrec	*by William, bishop of Norwich*
????	James (resigned)	*by the Prior and Convent of Castle Acre*
1221	John Hervey	
1286	Arnold de Lupo	*by the King*
????	Gilbert de Middleton	
1312	John de London	*by the Prior and convent of Castle Acre*
1328	Robert Godwyn of Syderstern	"
1349	Edmund Clerke de North Cryke	"
1349	John Atte Grene (exchanged)	"
1354	John Cordwaner	"
1366	Richard Pycot	"
1383	John Forester (Foster)	"
1404	William Balle	"
1404	John Goleth	"
1444	John Newgate	"
1444	John Synow	"
1447	William Crane	"
1509	Thomas Style	"
1529	Richard Bayly	*by the assigns of the Prior and Convent of Castle Acre*
1540	Thomas Leman	
1554	Thomas Markham	*by Thomas Duke of Norfolk*
1557	Richard Walker	*by Thomas Pepys gent.*
1581	John Hart	*by Fermor Pepys*
1583	John Hart	*by the Queen,*
1591	John Lindsey	*by Roger Pepys Gent.*
1617	Thomas Lynge	*by Richard Norton and Fermor Pepys*
1658	Thomas Howlet	
1666	Edmund Turner	*by Thomas Dyke and his wife Elizabeth, John Turner and Jane (nee Pepys) his wife*
1669	John Cleaver	"
1710	Thomas Donne	*by Robert Donne (churchwarden)*
1739	James Goodall	*by Lord Townshend, Lord of the Manor*
1768	William Fisher	"
1784	Miles Beevor	"
1785	Robert Orme	"
1786	Samuel Vince	"
1822	Thomas Scrimshire	*by William Ainge*
1824	Henry Goggs	*by Henry Goggs*